T0106392

Azubike Uzoka

GROWING UP, GROWING OLD

Chronicle of an Ordinary Life

iUniverse, Inc.
Bloomington

Growing Up, Growing Old
Chronicle of an Ordinary Life

iUniverse books may be ordered through booksellers or by contacting:

iUniverse
1663 Liberty Drive
Bloomington, IN 47403
www.iuniverse.com
1-800-Authors (1-800-288-4677)

ISBN: 978-1-4620-2079-9 (sc)
ISBN: 978-1-4620-2078-2 (e)

Printed in the United States of America

iUniverse rev. date: 07/18/2011

Dedication

To Mom, Dad, and Uncle Luke Chukwudebelu
In profound appreciation

Contents

Preface

Why should a personal chronicle of an ordinary life interest anyone else? I truly do not know. Why does anyone write? The simple answer is that I always have been compelled to write. In the 1960s, I wrote a beautiful love story, but the manuscript was lost during the Nigerian Civil War. Perhaps people do find it useful to read about the experiences of others. In his book *Healthy Aging*, in a chapter titled "Ethical Will," Dr. Andrew Weil encourages aging people to "share your values, blessings, life's lessons, hopes and dreams for the future." While writing this book, I found great encouragement in Dr. Weil's words.

Sometimes I wonder, is this story really about me or about us, that is, those of my time, circumstances, and generation? I have thoroughly enjoyed living with the pains and the pleasures through which one grows and I thought I should share the joys and the travails of living with others. In 1958, at the age of twenty-three, I wrote the following:

> Falter not with failure's distress.
> Nor yet scintillate with success.
> Both are no ends,
> Mere directions of new trends.
> In reaching for growth
> And enhancing worth.

Some years later, I came across President Theodore Roosevelt's assessment of himself: "I am only an average man but, by George, I work harder at it than the average man." Roosevelt may have claimed being average or ordinary, but his was certainly not an ordinary or average life. However, like Roosevelt, I have had to work harder than others for everything I've gotten, and I never win sweepstakes.

There are so many people to thank, both for my life and for this memoir. They include my parents, my entire family, my uncles and my aunts. My uncle Luke Chukwudebelu was an immense inspiration, always preaching about excellence and goodness. My beloved wife, Susan, dear companion and friend, has weathered the storms with me and shared in the fun too. Susan's support has grown with each decade, and she has been an untiring editor on this book and other projects. Her entire family members are all special people. I cherish the love of my nephews, nieces, and all the children on both sides of my family. My brothers, Okwudili and Chukwuemeka, and sisters Anne, Adaobi, Kate, and Stella, gave love and support. The children (Adaeze Susan, Uchenna Felix, Onyechi Leo, Anayo Kenneth, Ngozi Lillian and Arinzechukwu Stanley) and the grandchildren too are all sources of love. I am indebted to Hyacinth Obi-Keguna, my childhood friend, with whom I dreamed about life goals, some dreams fulfilled, some unfulfilled. The Nwachie family of Ossomala and Abala are truly decent people; spending my childhood in their home shaped the man I am today. There are so many other wonderful people, truly wonderful people, who have touched my life across time and race. I apologize for not mentioning them individually, but they are cherished. These include my teachers and my students from whom I learned so much—at various schools, places, and times. Professor Edith Elizabeth Lord, my great mentor; Professor Richard Carrera; Dr. Iris Bruel; and John Anowi were great teachers and motivators. I cherish these people. And I cannot forget my patients who taught me profound lessons about life, suffering, and dignity during such suffering, about creative coping strategies and the enormous strength of the human spirit.

My friend, the venerable Professor Israel Okoye, a dedicated scholar who kept encouraging me; his friendship and support transcended time and circumstance. Professor Rob Egwuatu, Professor Ifedioramma Nwana and Professor Aaron Gana are great scholars and friends. Claret Bob-Duru, Professor Patrick Obi Ngoddy, and my brother Chief Okwudili Uzoka kindly read through the manuscript at different stages of preparation and provided helpful insights. Scholastica Ogochukwu Borlin gave excellent secretarial assistance and never complained. I am indebted to Professor Obed Anizoba, professor of African languages at Nnamdi Azikiwe University, who kindly assisted with my Igbo language presentations. Any errors in this book are entirely and solely mine. I appreciate the assistance of Victoria Obianuju Ezejiofor, Librarian at Festus Nwako Library, Nnamdi Azikiwe University. I am grateful to the editors at iUniverse for their editorial assistance and helpful reviews.

I am grateful to all my family and friends for what you have given and for making my life worth living. I hope that I too have touched your lives in some meaningful measure. Finally, I thank the Creator, whose kindness has been boundless, truly beyond comprehension.

Azubike Uzoka
Awka, Nigeria
June 2010

Chapter 1

Early Memories

I don't recall being born. Someone told me that I was born at Uromi in the old Western Region of Nigeria, now in Edo State, on July 23, 1935. Somebody else said it was at Ughelli, at the time also in western Nigeria but now in Delta State. My father kept a small diary, which I saved until it was lost during the Nigerian Civil War, which definitely mentioned Uromi. It doesn't really matter. I have chosen to retain Uromi because it was the first I heard, it was written down, and I rather like the sound of the name. My father was a produce examiner for a multinational company. My mother was a housewife, barely fifteen years of age when I was born. She was a girl bride, as often was the case in those times. She had been married at about the age of eleven or twelve and spent two years of tutelage in the home of a townsman, Mr. Okwuosa, in Warri, Delta State, before joining her husband.

My mother's young age often created problems for me. When I joined the civil service in 1954, just before my nineteenth birthday, the house caretaker and my neighbors did not believe that she was my mother. When she visited, they would say, "You are enjoying oh!" meaning that I had acquired a girlfriend. I couldn't blame them. Mother looked so young and, more troubling, was extremely pretty. I was saved when my younger sister, Uzoamaka Stella, came to live with me, and our neighbors heard both of us calling our visitor "Mama."

I was Mama's second child. Her first, a male child, died due, I now believe, to her young age when she married. My first memories are of my mother; she had a smiling, beautiful face with which I fell in love, love that has endured beyond her lifetime. Mama was dainty, pretty, soft-spoken, and

1

gentle. Her name spoke of the standards of beauty and womanhood at the time. It was Oyibonanu, which meant that only a white man, or someone with the presumed qualities of a white man, was worthy of marrying such a beautiful woman. This was at the peak of the colonial days when "whiteness" defined excellence. Isn't it an irony of life that colonized peoples adopted that attitude?

In any case, my father did fit the bill. He was handsome and tall, so tall that he often had to bend down in order to enter most buildings of those days. And he had a good job. He had a standard-six (primary school) education, the highest level for most educated Nigerians at that time, and he was quite articulate. In fact, considering the language he used in his letters, I believe that so much was crammed into the school curricula at that time; the standard of education would seem to be more comprehensive than a high-school education is today. Dad even had a fair smattering of Latin! He undertook a training course and taught for a time in a primary school before becoming a produce examiner. He certainly was worthy of his young bride.

Even when I was past forty years of age and a grandfather myself, I still loved sitting on my mother's lap, and she would tease that I was about to break her tender, old bones. My children watching would sniff and say, "Mama's boy." Well, does anyone ever really grow up if parents, especially mothers, are still around? When my mother was visiting my family, and I came home past eight o'clock in the evening, she would point to the clock and say, "Papa Ada, why are you coming back so late? Why are you showing such bad example to the children?" She often addressed me as "Papa Ada" (father of Ada) whenever she was upset with me but used a more affectionate and endearing name "Azubikem" (my Azubike) at other times. Like a child, I would respectfully give her an excuse, such as "Mama, I was giving a late evening lecture to my postgraduate students. That's why I am home late." She would make no further comment but it would be clear from her countenance, that she was not satisfied with my explanation. All this would happen in the presence of my grown children. I never felt unhappy about these exchanges, however. In some strange way, they made me happy, happy to have my mother make me feel like a son.

My earliest and most-enduring childhood memory is of running about our neighborhood in the town of Baro in northern Nigeria, screaming that my mother was dying. That happened each time my mother had a long sneeze or a hiccup. The grownups in our neighborhood would tease me at all times and say, "Is your mother alive today?" or "Is your mother dying again today?"

I also have memories of tugging at my mother's clothes and wanting to go with her if she was going to the market and would not take me along. I remember her carrying me strapped on her back, even when I was more than five years of age; a relative would tend to my younger brother, who was about one year old. When I became an adult, mom would remind me of this and other oddities whenever I complained that one of my own children was too demanding.

Mother hailed from Akili, which was next to Atani, my hometown. It was one of a group of towns along the Niger River from the metropolitan town of Onitsha downstream, constituting a cultural area called Ogbaru. Her parents were farmers who fished as a side activity. I met my maternal grandfather when I moved to Onitsha after my primary-school education. I had good time fishing with him and two of his sons, who were at home as we were growing up.

Spending holidays at my grandpa's in Akili was always an exhilarating experience due to the experience of rivulet fishing. As the rainy season comes on, the rivulet tide begins to rise. Some rivulets from higher ground connect with the Niger, and fish that matured in their spawning lakes or other sources of water deep in the forest underbrush, would make their way back to the river. The villagers kept the routes of these seasonal rivulets under twenty-four-hour watch, with sentries alternating watch periods. Often, quite suddenly—at any time of day, but often in the early hours of the morning—the water would begin to flow toward the river. The quantity of water may have been very little to start with, just a trickle, yet the fish, especially varieties of catfish, would move along even if it meant they had to crawl in the mud. Then the catching would begin. Everybody would be required to be silent and make barely any movement. With no words spoken, the fish would be caught by hand or disabled with machetes and clubs and thrown into big basins or raffia baskets.

Excitement among the people would be at fever pitch, but they remained silent. People would make excited movements and gesticulate like a whole village of mutes. Each family group would catch so much of the big fish. The little fish were let go. Some types of fish were forbidden as food; for example, there was a catfish-like species called *ebbi* that has a fleshy flap that the townspeople call *ala* (breast). Any *ebbi* caught, was let go or given to migrant workers (*ndi isu*) and other people from the upland areas that did not have such prohibition. But everything was done in silence, except for the occasional sound of the machete or club. It was believed that undue noise would scare the fish back to their spawning sites. The catch would be followed by feverish cleaning of the fish while the fire was stoked for smoking it. And then there would be so much eating and nights of revelry, frolicking, and games. Rivulet fishing was always like a carnival.

Another fun activity was listening to tales by moonlight or sometimes around a fire. Most evenings, a good storyteller from the town or one nearby was invited to tell stories. The storytellers kept interest high by ending each night's episode with suspense; as a result, we would spend the next day wondering and speculating about the next part of the story. I learned later that these storytellers were paid for the task. Some of them were in great demand across the area and traveled from town to town, plying their trade.

Young and old people from different households within the section of the town called *Ogbe* (quarter) would gather around after evening meals to listen to wonderful stories about the exploits of men and women of valor and others about villains and what befell them. The really fun stories, at least among the children, took place in the animal kingdom. Often, these stories were about a tortoise that used his guile and trickery to win over bigger and stronger animals. However, sometimes the wily tortoise got burned by his own trickery. There was always a musical interlude or short musical piece accompanying the story; the audience would participate by singing choruses and occasionally by clapping their hands. Some of these songs became part of the repertoire of the children, who sang as they went about their daily activities. The children hurried to finish their evening chores so they could sit down and listen to the tales. Failure to finish one's chore was reason enough to be denied the pleasure of enjoying these exciting tales. That threat kept a lazy child on his or her toes. When there were no storytellers, there was always the moonlight play with all the young people frolicking around in groups or pairs, engaging in familiar games and inventing new ones.

Those were truly memorable times. I always longed to get back to Akili, especially because Onitsha, where we lived, was already a bustling cosmopolitan town with very little of the traditional ways. Those tales by moonlight covered a wide variety of moral and ethical themes, and they were clearly aids to child rearing and social engineering.

In my family, I was a wanted child. Among the Igbo, a major ethnic and language group that forms the larger population of southeastern Nigeria, every child is a wanted child. (In earlier times, the exceptions were twin babies because the birth of twins was considered an abomination.) As a child, I was quite pampered. I could always get my way, ate what I wanted, and was attended to by several houseboys. Our house was like a hotel, always bustling with visitors from the town and business people from afar. There were so many people around all the time. My recollection is that we lived a highbrow life. After work, Dad played tennis or checkers with friends, both white and black. There always was something cooking, and it seemed our kitchen was never closed. Most evenings, chicken or guinea fowl would be fried or roasted for Dad and his friends as they entertained themselves with their drinks after a few rounds of tennis. My special childhood treat was eating *garri* (a processed product of cassava, similar to grits) in cold water. I ate it with sardines placed

4

on top. I ate so much of the stuff that something of that early experience is still with me. Even now, although I am over seventy, if I ask for *garri* in the middle of an illness, my family will know that I am on the mend and on the path to recovery. My children tease me about this childhood food fad saying, "Papa, akpili gi, akpili garri na sardin aka ralo gi aka." (Papa, you have not overcome your peculiar childish longing for *garri* and sardines.)

My father loved his family, especially his brothers, and his extended family on both his father's and his mother's side. People complained that he spoiled them with excessive caring. He had one brother, Luke Chukwudebelu, by his mother and two, Ulasi Francis and Ezeweani Cyril, by his father's second wife. Mazeli, the wife of my great grand father Uzoka, hailed from a well-known Enekweizu royal family from Irefi village in Orifite town. She was the first wife of my great-grandfather Uzoka and was reported to be very rich.

Uzoka and Mazeli had several children but because they were twins, they were destroyed. As I stated earlier, in those days, twin birth was considered an abomination. After each birth of twins, the woman was kept outside the house for about twenty days, all her possessions (clothing, ornaments, cooking utensils, etc.) used during the childbirth, would be destroyed, and she was "washed clean" through traditional rituals. My uncle, Ulasi Francis, told me that the women who'd had the twins were so afraid after the event, they were usually very anxious to be "cleansed." Such was the power of beliefs and tradition. Uzoka had another wife who was only able to have one child, a girl named Uzoechi. (Her full name was Uzonwaechina, which means "may the path of childbirth never close.") There was truly anxiety to have more children in the home.

Uzoka and Mazeli expended a great deal of money consulting *dibies* (native doctors and diviners) in the effort to prevent twin births. But they only had more twins, as many as six times. In the end, they became fed up with the *dibies* and moved on with their lives. Then, unexpectedly, Mazeli became pregnant and delivered a single child, their only son Onedibie (my grandfather). In Igbo, the name Onedibie, short for Onedibie gwo zili nka, means "which native doctor now performed this successful outcome?" This was clearly a derisive comment on the efficacy of the native medicine men and sought to show that they had achieved a single birth without the help of any doctor. (Incidentally, twin genes were erased from our genetic heritage for more than one hundred years until my brother Okwudili's son, Chike Felix, had twin girls, one named Mazeli and the other named Oyibonanu, after our mother.)

Onedibie became a renowned wrestler. He didn't work. He did nothing but wrestle, purely for entertainment, and never earned any income from it. The story is that he would straddle the road and challenge passersby to a wrestling match. As a result, people who did not want to fight avoided that road and took side paths instead. Mazeli pampered and indulged him in all things and married him off quite early to two wives. However, he died in his prime following an operation to remove an inflamed appendix, and so his four children (my father and his siblings) were raised by their grandparents.

Because my father was much older than his three brothers, he served as the patriarch, taking care of them and other relatives. They visited our home quite often, bringing their problems and needs and also the filial warmth that Dad cherished. When they came, there was a lot of storytelling and lots of feasting as well.

In his old age, Uncle Ulasi, the oldest of the other three boys, was fond of telling one particular story. My father attended school in Onitsha, some eighteen kilometers away from Atani by road but several hours via a downstream boat ride. Making the return trip upstream often took almost a whole day, but the river was the main means of transportation at the time. Uncle Ulasi would say, "My brother was to come home after some years at Onitsha. We were so happy, so expectant. For me, time became almost stagnant, the days crawled. What will he look like? What will he be wearing? A thousand and one questions and scenarios rushed through my young mind. But none was like what I really saw or what happened."

At this point, Uncle Ulasi would stop and smile at no one in particular, his eyes looking down as he seemed to live through the experience all over again. Then he would continue. "At last the day came. News spread that my brother, Odili, had arrived. I ran to the river bank as swiftly as my eager legs could carry me, looking neither left nor right, with my heart thumping from sheer joy." There was another pause, and we listened carefully, waiting for the next bit, no matter how many times the story had been told and retold. "At the river bank," he continued, "I looked around for my brother. I did not see him. I recognized no one. Suddenly, this tall, strong man came out of the boat, made straight for me, and picked me up without warning. Too late for escape, I thought to myself, but I will not be an easy prey for this slave dealer! 'Help!' I shouted. 'Help me. He is going to sell me. I will not be made anybody's slave.' I fought as hard as I could to get away from his firm grip. The nightmare was real."

This was in the early twentieth century and some slave trade was still going on surreptitiously at the time, so my uncle's fears were well founded. At this point of the narrative, all of us would be rolling in laughter and anticipation, even though we knew what was coming next. One of us would urge him on, saying, "You were truly scared weren't you, Uncle?" He would nod vigorously in agreement and continue, "I struggled for some time until I heard my grandfather's reassuring voice. 'No my child,' Grandfather said,

'No, he is no slave dealer. This indeed is your brother, Odili.' It took some time for my pounding heart to slow down and for me to accept that this tall, big stranger was indeed my brother. With the realization, I relaxed and snuggled into his loving embrace. Then I held him even tighter than he held me. You can well imagine that I didn't let him out of my sight all through his stay. I followed him around wherever he went. I cried so much when he left."

Uncle Ulasi ended his story by saying in Igbo, "Nna yi solu ogonogo ooh, makwue mma nwoke." (Your father was oh so tall and handsome too.) Several years later, Uncle Ulasi came to my home in Enugu to pour libation on my freshly acquired Raleigh bicycle, offering prayers to the gods for my good fortune. But twenty years after that, when I bought a Peugeot 504, factory-fresh saloon car, he was displeased, saying that that was not a proper car for a university lecturer like me. A Mercedes Benz, he said, would be more appropriate. The libation he poured on the Peugeot car was definitely less spirited than the one he poured on my Raleigh bicycle.

My father named me Azubikem, meaning "my back is my strength," that is, his strength lay in his extended family, particularly his brothers and other close relatives. In Igbo culture, names often are associated with relationships—either with people or with the gods. In some Igbo areas, names also are associated with days of the week. With the prevailing custom, it would have been my father's grandfather, grandmother, father, or mother who would name his children. But by the time of my birth, they were all dead, so my father named his children himself.

My father had three wives and seven children, four daughters and three sons. I was the second in line. Anne was the first child. My other sisters are Kate (also called Goodluck), Adaobi, and Uzoamaka, the youngest. Another girl, named Nwinya, was born after Uzoamaka, but she did not survive. My two brothers are Okwudili Christopher (now Chief Ojiba, the Honorable Okwudili Uzoka, member of the Nigerian Federal House of Representatives) and Chukwuemeka Emmanuel, an attorney. My father's first wife, the mother of Anne and Kate, did not move with the family when my father's job relocated us to northern Nigeria. She and the two girls did not live with us in the north, and I did not get to connect with them earlier on. But the rest of my siblings lived together and missing them was the most painful part of my anguish, when at the age of seven I had to leave my parents' home and live with the Nwachie family, my father's relatives. (I will get to that story in the next chapter.)

It seems proper here to mention the strange ways my names have evolved. When I went to live with the Nwachie family, they registered me in school with their own surname and I was baptized with that name as well. My father complained when he saw my baptismal certificate, and they changed my surname to my father's first name, Odili. When I rejoined my family in Onitsha after primary school, I found that the whole family used Onedibie (my grandfather's name) as their last name, and so I registered in secondary school as Felix Azubike Onedibie. Two things propelled us to change the family name to Uzoka, my great-grandfather's name. First, when I joined the civil service, the European personnel were fond of calling me "Mr. One Dibie" (meaning "Mr. One Doctor"), a play on Onedibie, my last name. Mr. Greensill, who understood Igbo language quite well, enjoyed making jest of the name in that manner and I was truly uncomfortable with it, especially because many Nigerians also joined in.

I had an unexpected ally in my difficulty. My grandfather's only surviving sibling, Uzoechi, was unhappy that the family was known by her brother's name, Onedibie, rather than Uzoka, their father's name. She refused to be identified as N*wa* or *Umu-Onedibie* (child or children of Onedibie) since Onedibie was her brother. She often complained that the family name excluded her and gave her no social base in the town. Often in anger and with real vehemence, she would say, "Abuhom nwa Onedibie. Onedibie bu nwa nnem!" (I am not Onedibie's child, Onedibie is my brother!) She urged her nephews (my uncles) to change the family name to Uzoka or Anyaeji, their grandfather's name. Distressed with the Onedibie name myself, I was pleased to take her protest to my three uncles. We held a meeting and resolved that we should change the family name to Uzoka, to accommodate my aunt and, to my delight and relief, save me from the "One Dibie" jokes that had been following me around. What's in a name? What's wrong with a change?

My certificates show multiple names. My baptismal certificate reads Felix Odili Nwacheo (a misspelling of Nwachie). My primary school certificate reads Felix Azubike Odili. My secondary school certificate reads Felix Azubike Onedibie, while my Bachelor of Science and subsequent certificates read Felix Azubike Uzoka. In these days of certificate forgery and dishonesty (and ghost workers), I would have had a hard time proving that I am the three or more people reflected in my documents. Thank God, for age and retirement. The only thing I have to do to get my irregular pension, when it is paid, is to show my university appointment papers, which read Felix Azubike Uzoka, and then convince the personnel and bursary staff that the person standing before them is Felix Azubike Uzoka, that he is alive and is not a ghost.

Chapter 2

Away from Home

Learning to Work, to Take Responsibility, and to Have Courage

How does one learn to be courageous? I believe I learned how to be courageous in a most dramatic manner. How does one learn to work hard, to be responsible? I learned the hard way. As I mentioned earlier, I had a charmed life as a child with the world at my feet, pampered by my parents and extended family members. One incident changed all that and placed me in a situation where I had to cope on my own.

Several relatives would come to visit my family home, whether it was in Baro, Lokoja, Zungeru, or Gbagana, the various towns in northern Nigeria where Dad's job took the family. One sunny day, Mrs. Nwachie came to visit us in Baro. The niece of my father's grandmother, she was a native of Ossomala, a town twenty-three kilometers downstream from Atani. Ossomala is located on the eastern bank of the Niger and is the hometown of Nigerian legal luminaries such as Justice H. U. Kaine, Justice Francis Awogu, and the celebrated legal intellectual Attorney Fidelis Nwadialo, to name a few. (Mrs. Nwachie husband's family had settled in Ossomala; his parents had moved there from Abala, a town in Delta State. However, later in his old age, the husband returned to Abala, to take up the throne of his ancestors as the ruler. The Nwachies were then living in Minna, northern Nigeria.)

Everyone feared Mrs. Nwachie. My father did too. Perhaps he wasn't afraid but showed her the deep respect that was traditionally shown to older family members. Indeed, my father stopped smoking following Mrs.

Nwachie's rebuke. I still marvel at how it was possible for someone to give up an addiction merely because his great-aunt showed displeasure over the act.

My father had smoked on average about sixty to seventy cigarettes a day. He would begin the day by opening a sealed tin containing fifty cigarettes (usually the Guinea Gold brand). He would end up needing to add more from a packet of a less expensive brand of cigarettes (twenty sticks per pack). Although he often offered cigarettes and kola nuts as part of entertainment to his friends, I believe he smoked most of them himself. While he was a heavy smoker, he didn't smoke each cigarette to the end. Often, he would smoke only two-thirds or half of the cigarette and throw the rest of it away. Sometimes, the servants helped themselves to the leftover stubs; some of them choked and coughed furiously because it was their first attempt at smoking.

On one of her numerous visits, Mrs. Nwachie bellowed, "Who is smoking all the sticks of cigarette I see littered all over this house? Is it you Odili, the son of Onedibie? I do not want to see you smoking again. You are killing yourself by inhaling all that smoke. And you are not smoking with *foller.*" *Foller* was what the farmers and fishermen in the villages called a cigarette holder, which they made from wood. It was very popular with villagers. Those who used this holder divided a cigarette into three or four pieces and inserted each little piece into it at different times, both saving money and, unintentionally, also reducing the number of cigarettes smoked. In addition, smoking was usually a social affair among the farmers and fishermen; the holder was passed from person to person, thus further reducing the amount smoked by each one. Typically, each person would take a few drags and pass the *foller* to another person. If one individual indulged himself by smoking for too long, his friends would call him selfish and urge him to pass the *foller* on. My father did not use a cigarette holder. He smoked his cigarettes in one piece.

After Mrs. Nwachie's rebuke, nay, injunction, my father never smoked again. As a psychologist who has helped people give up nicotine or other substance addiction, I often have wished that the old ways persisted, and people had enough regard for their elders to change their habits because of the mere displeasure of a relative. Mrs. Nwachie had no formal education. Yet the fact of a somewhat distant familial relationship and seniority in age, gave her sufficient clout to effect such a change.

One day, unaware of Mrs. Nwachie's presence, I called out to one of the houseboys, asking him to bring me water to drink. Mrs. Nwachie overheard me and was furious. She asked with rage, "Who did I hear asking the servant to fetch water for him?" No one answered. I hid in trepidation. When Mrs. Nwachie shouted a second time, I again kept quiet. Then came her final threat: "Egbe ga ebulu onye kwulu okwu a ma'm juo ozo!" (A kite [small hawk] will devour the person who asked the servant to bring water, if I have to ask that question again!)

Young as I was, the idea of being devoured by a kite was quite real and frightening. Never mind that I should have known that a bird as small as a kite was unlikely to pick up someone my size. Never mind also the savvy exhibited by the current generation of young people. We weren't that worldly wise in my time. In addition, I did not grow up in a traditional Igbo setting where I would have learned the intricacies and nuances of Igbo idioms. Not wanting to be so savagely devoured, I said in a meek voice, crouching in a corner of the room, that I was the culprit. She said to me, "You are a firstborn male child (*Diokpala*), and you are behaving like a king already. A servant has to attend to you? You are being badly spoiled here! You are leaving with me to Minna."

She then upbraided my parents, saying, "Odili, you and your wife are raising a monster! Who is he to be served by a houseboy?"

That was the end of my charmed life. There was no more discussion, no input from my parents. Just like that, Mrs. Nwachie had given an order. My mother went into her room, where I found her crying silently. She dared not show her disapproval openly. I suspect my father, a doting father who had so much desire to be with his son, also must have cried in private. My greatest anguish was that I had to leave my siblings, Adaobi, Okwudili, and Chukwuemeka. Adaobi was three years younger than I was, Okwudili was four years younger, and Chukwuemeka was seven years younger. Chukwuemeka was just a baby when I left my family; I was about seven years old. The anguish I felt was indescribable. I cried so often.

I cried much of the time during the train journey to Minna, and not even the corned beef, sardine, and biscuits given to me by two World War II soldiers on the train provided enough solace. The banter among the soldiers didn't provide relief either, but I do recall their exhilaration. I don't know now where they were coming from or where they were going, but they mentioned Burma (now Myanmar) a few times, and they could have been part of the contingent that served there with the British army. They were boisterous, arguing and shouting among themselves. I believe they belonged to the same battalion or company. They talked about the merits of fighting the war on behalf of Great Britain and, the British Empire, the benefits they expected to attain after the war, and the prestige associated with being a soldier. They talked about their exploits, about those who had died, about how brave they were and how they were better than the *Oyibo* (white) soldiers. One soldier, a hefty man with broad facial marks, talked about how many people he had killed with his bare hands. In the midst of my tears, I was fascinated by their stories, and I thought that when I grew up, I would like to be a soldier.

11

Somewhere along the line, I fell asleep. I slept off and on, in-between snacks, until I arrived at Minna to begin life in my new home.

Once there, I found that several other children, male and female, were residing with the Nwachies. The tradition of farming out children to selected elders and families for proper upbringing was still quite strong. Mrs. Nwachie had acquired a reputation as a strict disciplinarian, and the elders said that no girl ever got pregnant under her care—that was her badge of honor. That was why many families sent their daughters to her for training. Her husband, Mr. Nwachie, seemed indifferent to things, while she exercised (to my puzzlement) an enormous amount of power in the home, within the neighborhood, and even beyond. She bellowed now and then that any girl who fooled around in her house was in for hell. It was said that she tested the girls' virginity every night by attempting to insert an egg into their genitals. The girls also were required to show her the cloth they used for menstruation every month (there were no sanitary pads then). Whether these stories were true or false I do not know, but people certainly believed that whatever she did worked.

Most of the boys and girls in the Nwachie household were bigger than I was and in upper classes, while a few were about my age. There were two "gospels" in the house: housework and church work. Every child had to be active in the church, and the boys had to be mass servers (later called altar boys or altar knights). We also had to be part of the church maintenance crew. We got up at 4 a.m. each day, and often went to bed at around midnight, if we were lucky. With the exception of Sundays, it was work, work, and more work. In the mornings we went to Gwari, a settlement some distance away from the main town, to get cassava, and we would peel the cassava before going to school. Often, we were late for school. We also had to carry materials for sale to Mrs. Nwachie's market stall and on our way back from school return via the market to bring back some unsold items. Mrs. Nwachie was a big-time trader in food items.

Garri preparation was a major activity. Each individual had his or her *garri* preparation regime. After peeling the cassava, we grated it into a mash by hand with the rough back of a metal grater. The grating process often left us with wounds on the edges of our palms. The older and stronger boys would tie up the mash in bags and then pile heavy stones on them to enhance drainage and drying. When the mash was sufficiently drained, we would strain it and spread it in the sun to dry. When it was fairly dry but still slightly moist and flaky, we would fry the cassava into *garri*. Each person had his or her own customers, who bought the prepared stuff from his or her basin. *Garri* preparation was only one of the family's many business activities. Besides *garri* making, there were various other chores associated with the house and Mrs. Nwachie's numerous business activities.

Meals were irregular and not what I was used to in my parents' home. Breakfast usually consisted of one small seed yam (*mkpulu ji*) eaten with fresh palm oil and sprinkled with salt and pepper. For supper, we often ate quite late at night, sometimes close to midnight. On some occasions, as one of the newer and youngest boys, I would be sent to hang around Mrs. Nwachie to let her see me and remind her that we had not been given our soup for the evening meal. Looking back now, I also imagine that the other children believed she had a soft spot for me. On seeing me, she would ask, "What is it?" Then she would add, "Oh, it seems you people have not eaten. I will soon come to give you your soup." Then she would immediately launch into another long conversation with her husband or one of the neighbors!

The children ate different soup from the soup enjoyed by the elders. That seemed to be the norm in township settings then, although it wasn't so in my parents' home. The elders' soup was cooked separately and was considered special. Anyone asked to wash the pot (*Ugbugba,* or *oku*, a clay pot) in which the elders' soup was cooked was considered lucky. That person would find a convenient place to start licking the pot dry before washing it. The thumb and index finger would be used to scrape out the remnants of the soup lodged in the top edges and bottom of the pot. There was usually very little left to actually wash. Truly, the leftover soup was quite delicious because it contained special ingredients that had congealed and become more concentrated. A good friend would come over to ask for some helping, reminding the lucky fellow that he or she enjoyed similar access when other people were given the pot to wash.

Our soup had large quantities of vegetables that, from a nutritional point of view, must have been healthy for us. The red unpolished rice (called *igbawale*), a lowly and cheaper brand of rice that was eaten mostly by poor folks but now is recognized to be very nutritious, was our regular fare. Often during the Sallah celebrations (Muslim festivals), the family was given several live sheep as gift. These would be slaughtered, salted, and sun-dried for preservation. Because the Nwachies, by tradition, did not eat mutton, which is forbidden in their Ossomala village culture, only those of us in the house who did not have such prohibition ate the meat throughout the year. Because of this, I developed intense distaste for mutton and, even now, I cannot tolerate the odor of it.

One of the privileges I enjoyed was that my parents would send some money for my upkeep, and Mrs. Nwachie would give me two or three coins for buying snacks during the school recess period. (*Anini* was then the smallest coin denomination.) I believe my father insisted on this after observing our feeding pattern in the house during one of his visits. There was another young man, slightly older than myself, who was a bully. Let's call him Andrew. He was about a year older than I was and much sturdier in physique. Gradually, Andrew began to force me to give him a large portion of my snack (usually *akara*, i.e., fried bean balls); I had to make do with a smaller portion. Because I was afraid of him, I did not complain. He threatened me at every turn. The situation got worse as he started to demand all my money from me as soon as we left the house for school, insisting that he was better able to make good buys. You can well imagine the portion of the snack I ate, once he did the buying. But I continued to suffer in silence. I am still not aware of how a relation of Mr. Nwachie, who was attending school in Onitsha but came up north on holidays, took notice of what was happening.

One day, on our way to school, after the bully had taken my pocket money again, we suddenly found young Master Nwachie behind us. He stopped us in our tracks and said the bully and I had to wrestle. In Igbo, he said, "Unu ga agba mgba." (You both will wrestle.)

I was scared stiff. But he meant it. He ordered us to put down our schoolbags and commence wrestling. I was petrified. Andrew was clearly delighted and eagerly came forward for the encounter. I balked. But Master Nwachie was unyielding. We wrestled or, more correctly, Andrew quickly brought me to the ground. I thought that was the end of the affair, and I made to get away, but young Master Nwachie said we had to continue wrestling. Again, I was thrown even before I knew the wrestling had started. We got up and were ordered to continue; it was a harrowing experience for me. At a point, however, something in me snapped. I do not understand, even today, the metamorphosis that occurred in me. I got up, stood my ground, and with one determined burst of energy picked up my adversary and threw him roughly to the ground. He got up and made to run away, but Master Nwachie was not to be denied his fun or, as I now believe, his lesson for us. He ordered Andrew back. Again, before you could wink an eyelid, I had him on the ground and pinned him down. Master Nwachie pulled me away. He wanted nothing physical beyond wrestling.

I do not now recall how many times we were put to this grueling but increasingly pleasurable event for me. Andrew, the bully tormentor, was in tears. I don't know what came over him. Perhaps he had expended so much energy in the early phase of the contest, or perhaps he had become overly confident and left his guard open. Or indeed, he wasn't as tough as he thought he was. In the end, Master Nwachie asked him to hand over my snack money to me. I do not recall whether we even made it to school again that day. He gave us a short lecture on good behavior and not hurting or cheating other people and went on his way. In this way, I regained my freedom from Andrew's tyranny, and I believe the experience has stayed with me all through life.

Andrew, the former bully, and I have remained friends, and even in old age, we joke about the event. He has remained somewhat of a forceful personality, but I believe that he was chastised by the experience and so his tendency to bully others was put in check. He had learned a lesson in the management and control of aggressive behavior. When I became a practicing psychologist, I often wondered how many children's lives are affected by incidents that either empower them as did mine, or engender feelings of inadequacy and fear that may persist throughout life. I shudder to think of what would have happened if I had continued to be beaten by my oppressor. In any case, I learned a major life lesson, that fear is a coward when confronted with resolve. The bully is tough only as long as the oppressed continues in fear.

There were many privations during my sojourn in Minna; there were also many rewarding aspects. For example, although I was one of the youngest, I had the privilege of being the one who frequently was asked to write business letters for Mrs. Nwachie. She had to keep in touch with her business partners in the far south. Her husband was a railway employee, and she was a big time fish and food trader. She also sold what was then called "illicit gin" (or *kai-kai*, *ogogoro*, or *akpeteshi*), that is, gin brewed locally from palm wine. It was subject to legal prohibition and many raids by policemen, who then bought the stuff when the raid was over! In fact, they drank the stuff right in our sitting room. I believe there was usually a tip-off by a policeman when a raid was contemplated. With the tip-off, action was taken to hide all evidence. The gin was transported in twenty-liter container tins by rail from the south of the country. The tins would have layers of very thick palm oil spread all over the tops, bottoms, and sides to camouflage them, and they were shipped alongside real palm oil containers. I doubt that the law-enforcement officials were actually fooled. Given the nationalistic fervor in Nigeria at that time as well as the affordable price of the "native" stuff compared to the British approved and imported brand, it seems clear that law-enforcement officials did not agree with the "white man's law" and were ready to keep the trade alive. It says something about law enforcement and perceived equity. One or two smalltime fries engaged in the trade would be caught now and again and shown around to prove that the police were active and performing their duty.

My auntie would always show me off as the one who wrote business letters that her business partners understood and never made mistakes. I wish I could find one of those letters to determine if she were correct. I am sure I must have made mistakes as I was only in standard four in primary school at the time. However, it was always a deeply rewarding experience to be singled out to perform that task. My handwriting was quite good then, with nice cursive flourishes, not what it has become now—largely illegible. Mrs. Nwachie would be ashamed of me if she were around now to see my handwriting, impoverished by carelessness, age, unsteady hands, and the luxury of typewriters and the computer on which I now write.

I am convinced that I became who I am, that I achieved my modest successes, because of the singular event of leaving home and staying with my great-aunt and her family. In the Nwachie household, you learned to do things for yourself, to be independent. And the elders taught by example because they too worked just as hard. I even learnt to cut my own hair, with two mirrors positioned so I could see the back of my head. Since leaving the Nwachie household in 1949, I have not been to a barber. Susan, my wife, now cuts the back for me and says I ought to pay her for the task. I tell her that I am already paying heavily in affection currency.

The strict upbringing and its associated work ethic have stayed with me. Why else would I enjoy doing house chores when there is household help and several grandchildren ready, or at least able, to do the job? Why does work give me such joy? In fact, I find physical work to be a respite from intellectual activity. I always want to be serving others, and being served makes me uneasy. Some people in the family refer to me as "okei ahu nfe," which means "a light-bodied elder." That nickname often is applied to an elderly person who jumps to get things done, rather than wait for things to be done. My relatives tell me, "You don't behave like a big man; like a professor." I guess I will never know what it is to be a "big man," or how to be one. I must be missing something.

Deep in my heart, I find myself thanking Mama-Nnukwu (Senior Mother), as my great-auntie Mrs. Nwachie was called, for taking me away and making a real *Diokpala* of me. How else could I have coped after my father's sudden death? Uncle Luke Chukwudebelu said to me, "Look, Azubike, you are now a man. You and I have to plan what to do with our family and you cannot afford to play around."

That was not idle talk. Just past my fourteenth birthday, my childhood did, in fact, come to an end. If I tried to play with the other young boys, my uncle would call me into the house, reminding me of my role and responsibilities. I resented this for a while but soon recognized that he was right and that playtime was over for me. I became a man before I was fifteen. More than two decades later, I came across James Dobson's excellent book, *Dare to Discipline*. Dobson insists that "there is security [for children] in defined limits." Other people, other cultures also have conflicts in childrearing: to restrict or not to restrict; to punish or not to punish, and how to do it; the limits of freedom and the essence of responsibility. These are the eternal challenges of the human enterprise of childrearing. I profited so much from the traditional "farming out" culture, and I truly wish the culture had been preserved instead of the present situation in which children are entirely the business of their natural parents.

Child Midwife

Another striking experience I had in the Nwachie household was to serve as a midwife. Mr. Nwachie had a second wife who arrived after I joined the household. The woman, named Oneje, had been married to a kinsman of Mr. Nwachie, but the man died before the consummation of their marriage. As custom had it, Mr. Nwachie inherited the brother's wife (*nkwuchi* in Igbo). Mr. Nwachie and his first wife, my great-aunt, also had only two children: Emmanuel and Veronica. It was thought that Mr. Nwachie ought to take another wife and have more children since his first wife was no longer having babies. So, the young woman arrived. She was rather on the short side, and we thought she was another young lady brought into the Nwachie household for training. After a while, it became obvious that she was our master's wife as she went into his room to spend some nights. There was a pattern of the women sharing "sleeping" nights with their husbands. It was traditionally determined and posed no apparent problems. Then the new wife got pregnant.

On that fateful day, all the people in the house were away, and Oneje and I were the only ones left. I cannot recall why this was so. The neighbors, who were some distance away from our house but within shouting range, had also left, and the closest people were more than a kilometer away. Oneje was heavy with child and was wobbling about with her stomach protruding unusually, sharply pointed in front of her. The prominence of her pregnancy was accentuated by her short stature. Then, at midday, she went into labor. She came out into the living room, spread a raffia mat (*Ute*), and stripped herself naked. That was my first sight of a naked woman, and I was taken aback. This was her first pregnancy but she seemed to know what to do. She had put water on the fire to boil, made a warm bath from it, and set it aside.

Then came the labor. She spread her legs and began to heave up and down in obvious distress. She was gritting her teeth and calling on God and the gods—"Chukwu eh, Chukwu Abiama"—to help her. A particular god or deity from her village of Ossomala, called Oji-Umugolo, was constantly on her lips. "Oji-Umugolo, Oji-Umugolo," she moaned continuously. "Oji-Umugolo, where are you? Come to my rescue. I have not offended you or the ancestors. I have not gone astray. I have not committed adultery. Oji-Umugolo-eh, no man but my husband has crossed my legs. I deserve your protection! Oji-Umugolo, I beg you to save me."

I stood transfixed. I didn't know what to do. After a while, she asked me to hold her back, and she spread her legs wider and started pushing. I was about nine years old and, at that time, there was no public education that would have equipped me with basic knowledge about birth or human anatomy. There was no home education either because sex was a taboo subject in the home. I was petrified. If one had grown up in a traditional village, one would probably have acquired a native sense about things. Unfortunately, the places where we resided were up and coming multiethnic small towns and townships (*Sabon Geris*, or "new towns") inhabited by numerous ethnic groups. Minna, Zungeru, Gbagana, and Baro, for instance, had such enclaves, with no dominant culture and with Western ideas compounding a discordant situation. I had no idea where babies came from. In fact, when it was all over and the other children asked me what had happened, I told them that she *excreted* the child!

I don't recall how long this frightening event took, but eventually a baby boy came out shouting. I believe the afterbirth also came out right after, and I thought it was another baby but it didn't look like a baby and didn't cry. The shouting by the baby scared me even more, and I made to sneak away, but Oneje asked me to stay with her. She asked me to get the kitchen knife, which she used to cut what I now know is the umbilical cord. I had to hold the baby (blood, slime, and all) while she did the cutting. She used the tepid water to clean herself, and she also wiped the baby clean. I do not now recall whether she actually bathed the baby, who continued to cry for some time.

We were done, and she was now cuddling the baby when the first of the family members came home. There was joy all round. However, the husband and other elderly visitors repeatedly upbraided Oneje for not indicating earlier on that she was going into labor. My auntie, the elder Mrs. Nwachie, called her *igbulukwu*, an Igbo word that means "a hardened mischief maker," for having a baby practically on her own. The word *igbulukwu* did not always have a negative meaning, however, because sometimes the elders would say that they meant a hardy or tough person, not a hardened one, and they would laugh. The young child grew to adulthood and became a banker.

For a while, I had nightmares about this event. When I now consider all the circumstances of the birth—including the use of the regular kitchen knife, which was not sterilized, to cut the umbilical cord—I begin to wonder whether germs have become more potent some generations later. I also acquired a nickname from this episode. They called me *one-ime*, which means midwife. When there was a pregnant woman around, they would say to her that if she needed a midwife in an emergency, she should consult me. Sometimes, I felt proud of this, but sometimes I felt embarrassed.

Finding Out: Childhood Curiosities

One of the characteristics I developed while I was with the Nwachie family was the sense of curiosity and exploration. This found its full expression when we moved to Kano, and we had a bit more free time. The *garri*-making was reduced in intensity, and life became somewhat easier. When in school, and we had some free time, we explored the environment extensively. We built toy motorcars from raffia stems and sold them to others, especially European visitors who found them attractive art pieces.

We also kept pet scorpions. We kept the scorpions intact; their stinging spikes were not removed. A process of native immunization by *mallams* (Hausa medicine men) made one immune to their sting, which was especially painful. I don't know why it worked but it did. We called the dark, huge dangerous species "railway scorpions" because we caught them along the railway tracks. Sometimes, we carried the creatures in our pockets to school to scare others, a macho thing. On one occasion, a whole class was called out into the open, and the boys were made to empty their pockets to see who was carrying the creatures in class. Each child caught with a scorpion received twelve lashes of the whip. Fortunately, it wasn't my class. I was carrying one of the creatures in my pocket that day!

In Kano, children of different ethnic groups traded jokes with each other. Friendship involved trading jokes. We called each other names, and these had no hurtful undertones or overtones. I would call the Hausa boy *arna* or *Kafiri*, meaning infidel or unbeliever, but more profoundly a worthless person. In response, he would call me *arna* or *nyamiri*, a bastardization of the Igbo words *nyem mmiri* (give me water), used as an abuse term. No offense was felt or expressed during these exchanges, which were taken as warm, friendly, banter. Adults also engaged in these exchanges; apparently, the children learned from them. Later, thanks to politicians in Nigeria, these jokes acquired hurtful undertones and overtones, thereby creating tribal animosities.

In Kano, I went to my first political rally. The Nigerian elder statesman and leader, Herbert Macaulay came to Kano in 1945. It was a real jamboree. He was the leader of a national political party. The town was agog, and we children had a field day running around. It was either on a weekend or the day was declared a public holiday as schools were closed. One of the young girls living with us broke her knee in the excitement; her kneecap popped out, and she had to go to the hospital for treatment.

One exploratory activity in Kano nearly cost me my life. I had been admitted to the hospital for some illness, perhaps a cough. I was fascinated by electricity. At the time, we did not have electricity in the Emir Road house in the *Sabon Geri* where we lived. I was fascinated by the way a single switch would bring the light on and off, again and again. At that time, the electric switches had a brass cover that could be screwed on by hand in a clockwise motion, rather than the steel screws that are now used to hold the plastic covers in place. I watched this magic on and on. One day, I decided to see what was inside the switch that performed this magic. I turned the cover around until it came off. Then I put my fingers in to examine the contents. The electric shock picked me up from my bed and threw me savagely on top of another sick person in an adjoining bed. I screamed in my fright. The whole hospital was in a huff. I was shouted at and abused and told that I had nearly killed myself and perhaps other people. "Idiot," "stupid," and "rascal" were the terms that were applied to me in quick volleys by different people. The management promptly discharged me from the hospital and sent me home. I believe I instantly recovered from whatever ailment I had! The puzzle about electricity remained with me for many years until much later when I took the time to read up on the scientific basis for the transmission of electric power.

My exploratory behavior had its origins early in my life, in my parents' home. In those days, we listened to music on a gramophone, a contraption with disposable pins that played breakable disks called gramophone records. Only the supposedly up-and-coming middle class could afford them. People, young and old, would come to our home and fill up the living room, with many more standing by the windows, to listen to the music. Some popular songs in our family record collection were "Zikki Nwa Jelu Oyibo" (Zik who went to the white man's country), an Igbo song about Dr. Nnamdi Azikiwe, a Nigerian nationalist; some Spanish and Portuguese rumbas, such as "La Paloma"; and two classical music records whose titles and artists I cannot now remember. I broke dozens of these records in the attempt to find out what was inside them that made the music.

More than the records, I was intrigued by the machine itself. The most popular gramophone had the brand name His Masters Voice (HMV) inscribed on the body. The logo was a dog sitting with a dignified pose. I thought the dog was the agent that did all the singing. I could not understand how the dog could do all that singing that came from the gramophone when our family pet dog named Siddon-look (Pidgin English for "sit down and look") could not speak a word in English or Igbo. Perhaps, it was a special breed of the white man's dog that had such special skills. On two occasions, I actually yanked my father's gramophone apart to see this special dog. There was no dog. (It did not occur to me to imagine what the dog would be eating while it was entombed in the machine!) In consternation over my exploits, my mom would say, "Your father will kill both of us today. You just wait and see!"

Well, I did not get beaten or even scolded. The truth is that I never saw my Dad flog anyone or ever heard a scolding word between him and Mom.

So, her statement was the usual situation of a mother using father's status and image to keep the children in check. When he came home and heard what I had done, Dad would cuddle me and say, "Dimkpam, i mego kwa tata?" meaning "My great fellow, have you done it again today?" He would then pick me up, hug me, and throw me up in the air. He laughed when I told him I was looking for the dog that did the singing. I believe I was past six years old, clearly spoilt. He took his time to explain the logic of the machine to me, pointing to each component and explaining its function. I didn't quite understand the explanation, and I didn't quite give up the notion that the dog had something to do with it. I thought that grown-ups have strange ways of explaining simple things. But if Dad said the machine worked on its own, it had to be so. Dad often enjoyed telling visitors to the house of my search for the singing dog, and they would all laugh over it. Mom never stopped repeating this story anytime I complained about one of my own children damaging some gadget.

Chapter 3

Premonitions and Future Events

When I was a child, I could foretell events. It was uncanny. This is a mystery I have pondered and lived with throughout my life. It remains a puzzle still. This skill became quite prominent while I was living with the Nwachies. On several occasions, I would tell them of an event that was going to happen and, in fact, it would happen, just as I'd said it would. If I told them that someone was coming to Minna from a town in the far south, at least some six hundred kilometers away, the person would arrive shortly afterward. This happened so many times that it became routine for them to ask me, "Who is on the way to Minna [or Kano] today?"

However, many of the predictions were about death. If I said that a death had occurred and that we'd hear about it soon, a report matching the details I'd stated would be received immediately. It was uncanny, and my premonitions were far too frequent, consistent, and correct to be mere coincidence. The family became quite troubled about this, and they held me responsible for the events I predicted. They gave me a hard time. At one point, they even got me to sleep with the husband or wife to prevent me from dreaming some of the things I would foretell. I always felt compelled to announce these predictions, even though I knew I would be harangued for doing so. I doubt that I would have escaped lynching today, when children are hounded as "witches" for unusual behaviors in parts of Africa and elsewhere. The Nwachies invited my father for discussions on the matter. Then they brought in a variety of native doctors and medicine men and even a man who said he got his magical powers from India. One of his magical preparations was a gourd tied with red cloth that was hung in front of the room where the children slept. Something happened, however, to change the family's negative attitude about these events.

Mr. Nwachie was a member of the railway staff and also of the union. He had quite a reputation and much clout. Once, a steel component he was working on fell on his hand and cut off three or four of his fingers. The fingers were sutured back on but remained straight. I believe three of them could not bend anymore. He used to play the guitar before the accident (with only one tune in his repertoire) but was unable to do so after the accident. Every evening, he would apply hot treatment and shea-butter oil (called *okuma*) to the fingers. The accident was a badge of honor that seemed to give him added prestige in the work place.

In 1946, he was due for annual leave. He announced with pride that we were going on holiday to their hometown, Ossomala, in the south. In addition, due to a recent promotion, he had been allocated a second-class compartment on the train rather than the third-class one he'd used in the past. At that time, the second-class compartment, a somewhat private space, was a prestige matter and quite a big to do. Four days before our departure, I went up to Mrs. Nwachie and announced,

"We are not going to travel by the train reserved for us because some other people are going to use the train. We won't be traveling now." They were furious and told me, "Bulu amosu yi pua ebe a!" (Take your witchcraft somewhere else!)

The very next day, a message arrived from the railways, announcing that the space earlier allocated to Mr. Nwachie had been taken up by a team of European personnel who had arrived to make repairs on the rail line or undertake some survey. A new date for our trip would be set in the future. There seemed to be no end to the misery I suffered for the next two days. Mr. Nwachie had prepared himself and the family back home in Ossomala for his journey home and was visibly shaken by the disappointment. He moved about the house upbraiding everybody at the railway for forgetting his extensive contributions to that establishment, vowing to get back at somebody for this "insult." Then I bore the brunt of his anger, after he was finished with haranguing the railway authorities. "What was my sin," he wondered aloud, "for taking in Odili's boy, Azubike, for upbringing? Where did I go wrong?" he asked repeatedly in a voice full of self-pity and thinly veiled anger. He blamed his wife for bringing me there and announced that his permission had not been sought before I was dumped in the house. There was no peace in the home. But all that was soon to dramatically change.

On the appointed date, the train took off with the repair experts on board. Early the next morning, however, news came that the train had been involved in an accident around a place called Geti. It was the worst accident ever experienced by the Nigerian Railways, and several people had died. I was called into the center of the living room to be gazed at, celebrated and cuddled, and so on. I was asked how I knew we were not going to travel by that train. Of course, I did not know how I knew. I just felt compelled to say what I knew. All sorts of rituals followed. They killed a chicken and sprinkled the blood on my feet and did other things I can no longer remember. A goat was slaughtered in celebration. They said I had saved the family from imminent death. I did not understand what it was all about, but from then on, nobody troubled me about the premonitions. Instead, I was courted and treated like some great prize.

These premonitions continued for some time. When I returned to Onitsha to stay with my uncle, my mother, and my family and attend secondary school, some native doctors were brought in to stop the premonitions. The last one was a Yoruba man with distinctive facial marks who made cuts on my skull and rubbed in some kind of concoction. As I began to get serious with school, the episodes decreased, and I discovered that I had an eidetic memory. I was able to recall my notes and the books I read without looking at the material. For instance, I could see in detail all of Shakespeare's *Julius Caesar* or *As You Like It* or *Twelfth Night,* with all the marks and comments I'd written in the book as if the book were open. They looked like photos or slides. All I had to do was to close my eyes, and I would see the whole text, page after page. Years later when I joined the Eastern Nigeria Theater Group, also called the Ogui Players in Enugu, I became the unofficial prompter and would remind others of their lines. All I had to do was close my eyes and the page would emerge, clear and distinct.

The earlier premonitions and subsequent ones have remained a puzzle. For instance, how was it possible for me to name each of our six children with gender-specific English names *before* they were born? In each of six times, I knew (and stated) the sex of the unborn baby ahead of time. I had the right to give the English names since, by tradition, one of the elders—my mother, uncle, or my wife's parents—would give the Igbo names. I named the first girl Adaeze Susan, and I was right: a girl was born. (I desired a girl and my wife couldn't understand why. "Don't everyone, especially men, always want a male child, at least at the first instance?" she asked.) Then I named boys three times in a row, and I was right: Uchenna Felix (who passed on at age four), Onyechi Leonard, and Anayo Kenneth. Then I named a girl, Ngozi Lillian, and was right again. She was interesting. When we patted Susan's belly as the baby heaved up and down in the womb, obviously playing as well, Susan kept insisting the baby "kicked" in the womb like a boy. I insisted it was a girl and named the unborn baby Lillian. And a girl she was. She now has five of her own children, but pretty as she is, she sure had some male energy and was a real tomboy when she was growing up. The last boy was warm and handsome Arinzechukwu Stanley, who gave us a wonderful seven years and went back to the Creator.

I named all six of them while they were still in the womb. And this was at the time when there was no ultrasound and no routine sonic imaging in the medical field.

When I was predicting these events, I did not have the sense of seeing things or feeling any different or powerful. My actions were just matter-of-fact behavior. Can one really anticipate or predict the future? Someone who heard the story joked that my "magical gift" was truncated by the interventions of the various medicine men who were "foisted on you when you were young, or perhaps it was really your growing-up and immersion in the wider social life and your sins that caused the diminishing of the process." He joked that I would have done much better in life if I had taken up fortune telling as a profession. Neither of his explanations seems sufficient for what is still for me a perplexing phenomenon. In any case, he was probably right in saying that this characteristic "diminished" because even now I have an uncanny intuition about things and events. A consequence of my experience, was that early in my adult life, I prayed against events, especially if in anger, I had felt bad about someone or had expressed a hurtful emotion. I prayed because instinctively, perhaps superstitiously, I feared it might come true. Another consequence is that in my clinical practice, I am able to listen with great empathy to my clients, especially young people, when they report unusual experiences that are not easily explicable in terms of the routine cause and effect logical sequences of everyday events. I also empathize with the feelings that accompany such experiences.

Chapter 4

Secondary School and Other Beginnings

I had no problems in primary school. However, despite one double promotion, the various transfers from one town to another cost me school time. Sometimes, my surrogate parents would be posted to another town in the middle of a school year, which prevented me from completing the current academic year. Once, I had to repeat a year that I had not actually failed. Secondary school was fun. But let me start from the beginning.

When I was in primary school, in standard five, my father decided that I would undertake my secondary schooling in Britain. Sending one's children to study in England was the big thing then; maybe it still is. Dad's friends were sending their children overseas for secondary school education. He dismissed my suggestion that I take the entrance examinations to the prestigious King's College and St. Gregory's College in Lagos. He was adamant that I should be educated in Britain.

My father also wanted to send his younger brother Luke Chukwudebelu to Britain for further studies. Luke had just returned from the army. I believe he was in East Africa when the war ended. While in the army or immediately after, he passed the London Matriculation Examination, an equivalent of the intermediate Bachelor of Arts degree (Associate in Arts degree). He was a brilliant man. Later in life, he obtained a Bachelor of Arts degree in history (with honors) from the University of London as an external candidate. He was the first person from my hometown to obtain a university degree. He and others like him recognized that they were following in the footsteps of renowned Nigerian scholars like Professor Chike Obi, a well-known professor of mathematics. Such persons had studied at home for their degrees and excelled. Luke Chukwudebelu eventually became the principal at Modebe Memorial Grammar School in Onitsha.

There was some disagreement between the two brothers, my father and Luke Chukwudebelu. I was never able to ascertain what it was. However, when they resolved the disagreement, I was in standard six, the final year of primary school, at St. Paul's Catholic School in Ebute Metta, Lagos. My father asked my uncle to wait and travel with me. The arrangements were made. My suitcase was bought and filled with appropriate clothing. We were to travel by sea, which was then the only mode of regular transportation. After my standard-six examinations, I was told to travel to Onitsha. I didn't know why because my family had been residing in the north of the country. One of the "modern" popular modes of road transportation was by Armels transport, a lorry in which the front section behind the driver was made into a second-class "luxury" compartment. It was tight and provided no comfort at all. This was a long and tedious journey, but it was the best available. I arrived in Onitsha and found my uncle Luke Chukwudebelu, my mother, and my siblings huddled in a two-room living arrangement. I was puzzled. What were they doing in Onitsha? And why were they in such reduced circumstances? Poverty was clearly written all over the environment. And where was my father? I rattled off these questions in quick succession.

Everybody welcomed me warmly, but I sensed some strain in the air. I asked Uncle Luke directly, "What is happening? What are you all doing in Onitsha and where is my father?" He was evasive and merely said, "Eat first and we will talk. There is time enough to talk. You have a lot to tell us about Lagos." After I had finished eating, with tears rolling down his cheeks, he said, "My brother is dead. "

"Which of your brothers?" I asked. I asked because he had three brothers. With more tears streaking down his face, he blurted out, "Your father."

I was dumbfounded, but I held him and consoled him, even though it was my father who had died. He kept sobbing, and I too broke down in tears. Other family members also started crying. When we regained some composure, I asked, "Aren't we going overseas anymore?" I doubt that Uncle Luke actually heard me because he neither responded to the question nor referred to it in subsequent years. I wonder if my childish desire for overseas travel had momentarily transcended my grief for my father. I grieved for my father from then on, of course, over the loss of his loving presence, made more painful because of the penury in which we had to live.

My father had some pension money that was due to him, and that was another event. Many times, some extended family members descended on our home wanting to know whether the gratuity had been received and to demand a share of it. One day, when they arrived, an elderly aunt of ours, Madam

Obiora who had substantial clothing business, was invited to the meeting. After arguments and the possible allotment had been agreed upon, she said to the family members,

"We have now agreed on how to share Odili's gratuity. Now let us discuss how to share the upbringing of the children. Remember, they will all go to school and to good schools, including college."

None of them seemed ready to pay school fees, and so they abandoned their claims to the gratuity and left. In the meantime, food was sparse. Many times we had to go fishing to provide ingredients for the soup. Clothing was sparse and truly poor. My mother, formerly a pampered housewife, soon turned to preparing and selling cassava. She had acquired a significant quantity of disposable goods and merchandise and sent them down from the north, hoping to begin a business career. But everything was appropriated by a relative of ours. He claimed that the material had belonged to his brother (my father) and that, as widow, my mother had no right to it. For some time, this event caused considerable squabbles within the family; my mother refused to have any dealings with the man until I intervened and persuaded her to forgive him. In fact, much later on, the man—who squandered whatever money he made from my mother's goods and was living in poverty—died in her arms. Prior to his death, he told my mother to plead with me to look after his family. I have done so.

Fortunately at that time, there was a building boom in Fegge, a suburb of Onitsha, and I took on odd jobs as mason or carpenter's assistant to earn some income to help the family. I carried blocks and delivered sand to the masons and planks to the carpenters. I welcomed any odd job that paid something at the end of a working day. Sometimes, I worked for half a day since I had to go to school. It was truly rough, particularly for someone with my background, a veritable grace to grass situation. For two full years, I went to school barefoot because we could not afford the canvas school shoes, but thankfully the school authorities were not too particular at the time. Their concern was with the academic work, not fancy dressing.

My uncle Luke Chukwudebelu was teaching at Zik's Institute, Onitsha, and he enrolled me in that school. For a Lagos boy, a city boy who had his eyes on the reputable King's College or St. Gregory's College, this was a great letdown. Zik's Institute was a good school, however, and produced high-quality students. But the situation was certainly far from my dreams. Its reputation as a typing school, meant for typists and secretarial personnel, did not fit in with my dreams. Students from other schools often teased us about being in an inferior school. Furthermore, the knowledge that, but for my father's death, I would have been studying in Britain, made the situation unbearable.

After a semester or so, I opted to drop out. My uncle, a compassionate and loving person, did all he could to persuade me to continue, but I was adamant. I chose tailoring as a career. I had a distant uncle named Enweluzo who was a tailor. I used to spend time in his workshop and I liked fixing buttons and using the sewing machine. Besides, London-trained tailors were in vogue and I believed that if I worked hard enough, someone might be willing to send me to London to perfect the art. (The overseas travel dream was still alive.) I had worked as a tailor for about seven months when Uncle Luke called me to his side. He was a loving and deeply religious man who would shed tears over any distress. He said to me, "Why tailoring, Azubike? Schooling is the best thing for you."

I didn't budge but quickly sought to get him on my side by suggesting that I was saving the family expenses. I said, "You know the other children need help. If I perfect my tailoring skill, I will be able to assist in their upbringing."

He did not take that bait, however, and argued, "Azubike, you too need education. And what will I tell my brother when I meet him in the spirit world, that his first son is a tailor? You know the reason I put you in Zik's Institute. It was so that I will be able to pay your fees, or plead for deferment if I could not, or have them deducted from my salary. Please go and find another school and enroll, instead of the tailoring you are now engaged in."

I hesitated for some time because I had started to like tailoring. That was when tailors were real tailors, not fancy fashion designers. Anyway, after a number of reminders by him and in sympathy with his obvious distress, I went out in search of a school. I went to Metropolitan College, Onitsha, which was organizing examinations for the second-year class. I took the examination and came first. The school manager, Mr. Afubera, was excited and said to me,

"Nwanunwa, i na ma kwa akwukwo; nne gi o ga kwunwu kwa ugwo akwukwo gi?" (Child, you are brilliant, but will your mother afford your school fees?)

I replied that I did not know. And truly, getting my school fees would be a troublesome matter. Many times, I was obliged to stay away because I could not pay the fees. Anyway, after reflection, the school manager said to me, "Baa na class." (Go into class.) Thus began my secondary-school education. My uncle was happy that I gave up tailoring. For a while, I combined tailoring with schoolwork, but gradually schoolwork became preeminent.

The school was pleasant but rough. It had some very good teachers. But a number had only secondary school education themselves, and some of them were not very good. Unfortunately, Wilson Onuigbo, an excellent mathematics teacher who eventually became a distinguished professor of medicine and an astute scholar, was just leaving the school as I was entering.

My first mathematics teacher was decidedly bad and created in me distaste for mathematics that has lasted throughout my life. Later, we had wonderful mathematics teachers, including M. S. C. Okoye. For me, however, the damage was already done. I hated mathematics. I tell Adaeze-Susan, who has a degree in mathematics from the University of Nigeria and an advanced degree in geophysics from Georgia Tech that she has compensated for my weakness.

There were other excellent teachers in other areas. John Ibeziako, who taught English language and literature, later became the accountant-general of Eastern Nigeria. Vincent Ikeotuonye taught us geography, and a wonderful history teacher, K. C. Ifeora, made history come alive. He made learning so much fun that nobody wanted to miss his class. He was a tall and handsome man with a dignified carriage. If the subject were Russian or British history, his lucid and dramatic descriptions, even when the presentations were brief, would make the Victorian and Romanov courts come alive with all the intrigues, and fun.

School was a great time, generally, but I didn't like the meals. Many times we found insects in the *akara*. I hated that and would rather go hungry. It was the same with the beans. The cooks took no pains to remove the weevils that infested the beans. Some of the boys didn't mind and gulped down their meals with relish. They even ate the food of those of us who were being finicky, joking that the weevils were added protein, comparable to another insect called *aku*, which many people ate, roasted or raw. What, they would ask, was the difference between these insects and the tiny crayfish that we all ate? Those insects reminded me of an old aunt in Onitsha in whose house we once spent a holiday with my parents. She yelled at any child who was picky about what was in the soup. When cooking, she washed only the outside of the dried fish and did not open up the fish to see if there were maggots inside, as there usually were. If you saw fish maggots or the mature insects (called *nna*) floating in the *nsala* (fish soup) and acted as though you were uncomfortable, she would shout at you, saying, "Bia nwa, ne nni libe, nna di na azu bu azu. Okwa azu ka nna ne li?" (Get on with your meal, child. The maggot [or insect] in the fish is also fish. Is it not fish that the maggots themselves eat?)

Some logic! Of course, if we had vegetable soup, the creatures would be hard to detect. I enjoyed meals only when we had fresh fish soup. She prided herself on her good cooking. The grand old lady, we understood, used to be quite finicky about these things when she was younger, but with old age and bad eyesight she had become complacent. I was so happy when that holiday ended.

The weekends at school were good. My mother took pains to bring me *foofoo* (made from cassava or yam), and I and my friends delighted in "fighting" over the food, as we did also when other parents brought in food. A couple of the boys had the incredible ability of swallowing very large morsels of food. Such lumps, almost the size of two joined ping-pong balls, would go down their throats with a loud noise, accompanied by the rise and fall of their large Adam's apples, their eyes popping out, and occasionally tears. To ensure equity, we decided that everyone had to show the morsel of *foofoo* he'd taken before dipping it in the soup.

All of us looked forward especially to my mother's cooking. She was an excellent cook and her *Ogbono* soup was especially tasty. With my mother, there was no hurrying with cooking. Cooking was an art to her. When you thought her soup was done, she would say that the simmering time was yet beginning. Even when gas and kerosene became available, she still preferred cooking with wood. At one point, she would reduce the fire to allow the soup to simmer, with small bubbles shooting up in the soup as it browned. Her baking was also great, and visitors to our homes in Zungeru and Baro often took a helping of the various items she prepared.

In school we were all quite boisterous and friendly, sharing not only food but also our few belongings. To me, bonds of friendship formed in secondary school appear to be quite unique. In my experience, primary-school relationships and university relationships rarely result in such lasting bonds. In adult life, I am amazed at how these secondary-school relationships have retained their warmth, fondness, and simplicity. Perhaps this is because in primary school, people have not become mature enough for lasting attachments outside the family. In secondary school, they have matured enough to establish friendships without the grownup airs that come with university-level studies.

Once, for example, I needed to conduct an urgent banking transaction. My branch could not execute the transaction and referred me to the regional office of the bank. When I got to the regional office that Monday afternoon, I was told that the matter had to be handled by the regional manager. But on Mondays, he did not entertain visitors after 2 p.m. under any circumstance. I had traveled over seventy kilometers, and it seemed such a waste of time to have to repeat the journey all over again. When I pleaded with the bank officer, he said, "Sir, even if his mother comes, he will not see her once he has gone into this meeting."

I thought he was exaggerating, but his meaning was clear. I asked for the regional manager's name. It was Ginger Eke. The name rang a bell. I asked whether Ginger Eke was from Afikpo town, and the officer said yes. I felt great excitement. In secondary school, a Ginger Eke was my classmate, and he was from Afikpo town. In school, we traded nicknames. We called Ginger *Enyi Offia* (bush elephant), and one of my nicknames was *Sofa* (meaning "follow them," a nickname I earned from not catching up in a relay race). I took my business card and wrote his nickname, an abuse we'd traded in school, and my own nickname. There was a chance that I was right. If not, the fellow would just think that some crazy nut was playing a game. There was nothing to lose. The officer agreed to take it up to him, although he said to me in Pidgin English, "Oga, i no go work." (Sir, this won't work; the note will have no effect.)

But the effect was electric and put the whole office in a huff. Ginger abandoned his meeting, came rushing out of his office, and in the presence of everybody there, pulled me up in a bear hug, shouting familiar abuses at me like some secondary-school boy. He was much larger than I was. In fact, his size was the reason we called him *Enyi*. We hadn't seen each other for over two decades. We shouted and jumped about, forgetting that we were in an office and forgetting all protocol. It seemed like only yesterday that we had been in school, romping around, loving life, being our natural and carefree selves, unencumbered by fretting egos. Ginger held up his official engagement for about thirty minutes while he attended to me, with all relevant staff commandeered for the effort. He did not want me to leave. I had to promise to be back soon for him to set me free. The warmth of the secondary-school relationship conquered all protocol and transcended the inviolable routine.

Sports always generated great excitement in our school. Usually, the Empire Day annual sports event was preceded by inter-house competitions that determined the best performers who would represent our school. Empire Day was held all over the British Empire and in all British territories. These games now are called the Commonwealth Games. I was good at the hundred-yard dash and took the lead in some relay races. I often won those competitions. But today, some may consider the prizes paltry. They were usually small metal buckets, bars of soap, exercise books, and pencils. The top prize was the highly prized, refillable Parker pen.

Sports provided opportunities for much camaraderie among the students and welcome relief from academic work. It was also time for teasing and name-calling. For example, this young man named John Agagaraga was a high jumper and very good at it too. He was from the Ijaw ethnic group that is spread over the coastal areas of the Bayelsa, Rivers, and Delta states in Nigeria's oil-rich basin. During competitions, his kinsman would shout at him, urging him on. But those calls often evoked much laughter from the crowd of students, teachers, and other spectators because he had difficulty with some letters, especially J and H. He would shout at John, "Zohn Agagaraga, zomp ayer" rather than "John Agagaraga, jump higher!"

The young man was known as "Zohn" throughout his stay in school. Very few students called him John. He didn't like it, poor fellow. Much later,

I learned about the source of some of the young man's difficulty. Most Ijaw people refer to themselves as Izon, not Ijaws, a name given to them by the British. The British often created pronunciations that were easy for them without taking into account people's preferences or sounds. For instance, even today, people in Onitsha refer to their city as Onitcha or Onicha, with the sharp "tch" sound instead of the "sha" sound. Members of my own cultural group use Ogbahu, but the British used Ogbaru, with "r" replacing the "h," which has persisted in official usage. People in Asaba in the Delta State insist that the proper spelling of their town is Ahaba. However, the British spelling, Asaba, is still used in official and public parlance.

In school, a boy named Peter Mgbaronye was supremely intelligent. I never saw him study once. But he always came first in examinations and eventually was the first in our class, I believe, to become a university graduate, an architect. Peter ended up as the chief architect of Imo State. When I got to know his family, I realized that intelligence was in his pedigree. Peter answered the question of genetics versus environment in a manner that remains a bias with me in the ongoing debate on intelligence. Peter was the most distracting person in class. Lively and full of fun, he touched and tweaked fellow students, making funny, low-voiced comments when the teacher wasn't looking. The other students would be caught laughing and sometimes were punished for disturbing the class. Yet Peter listened enough not only to pass his examinations but also to come first in all of them. I do not know if he even bought textbooks, and he was not bothered if you did not give him your own to read. He would merely shrug off any refusals. He did not even have a lamp for night study and when I got to know his family circumstances, I realized that this was not because of penury. He came from a family that was reasonably well-to-do. He just did not think it was necessary to buy books or own a lamp. Later I found out that his siblings were just as intellectually gifted as he was.

We were all quite adventurous, and some of us got into youthful exploits outside the school. Peter was part of our exuberant group. One particular activity that held our interest was going to listen to cases at the Customary Court in Onitsha, then called Native Court. In civil proceedings, such courts did not have lawyers or prosecutors. The judges listened to both parties to the dispute, asked relevant questions and rendered their judgment. One case held our attention, and we tried to attend court sessions whenever we could. The case involved a young girl and a boy, both in their teens. The girl claimed that the young boy had put her in the family way.

In one of the court sessions, the young girl was put to very intense questioning. One of the judges hearing the case, an old gray-haired member of the court, was apparently trying to establish her responsibility. He asked her, "Did he force you to have sex with him?" His questions were rendered in unfettered, explicit, and graphic sexual language that always created a stir and bouts of laughter by the spectators. The girl's halting answer was, "He begged me and begged me before I agreed." The court member kept questioning. "Did he force you into bed?" The girl said no but repeated that the young man begged her for a long time before she agreed to sleep with him. The judge then asked where the activity had taken place. She said it was in the boy's home. He asked, "Did he force you to go to his home?" The girl said no but repeated that the young man kept begging and begging and that was why she went to his house. The proceedings continued with more detailed carnal questions: Were you sitting or standing during the act? Was it on a mat or on the father's bed? How many times and on how many days?

The final questioning was most troubling for the young girl. He asked her, "Did you enjoy the act?" The girl kept silent. After repeated prodding, which sounded threatening, the young girl in a barely audible and quivering voice said, "The first time it was painful."

"Aha," said the judge gleefully, like someone whose trap had caught a valued animal. Rubbing his palms in sheer delight, he continued, "Then why did you continue to go, if it was painful?" The young girl had no response this time around, not even with continued prodding. She kept her head bowed and her eyes fixed to the floor. The judge charged on. "So, after the first time it wasn't painful anymore? You began to enjoy it, and you couldn't keep off. He wasn't begging you and begging you anymore. You see, that's why you got pregnant!"

The raw, erotic language that characterized these questions and comments evoked shouts and laughter from the large audience in the courthouse. Sometimes, even the other judges abandoned protocol and joined in the revelry, laughing boisterously, making nonsense of the court orderly's shouts of "Order, silence! Order, silence in court." When things simmered down, the head judge summarized the panel's position saying, again in erotic language, "You left your father's house and went to a boy's home to have sex with him, not once but on several occasions, clearly enjoying every bit of it. Now you are blaming him for your pregnancy because he begged you and begged you. That is no excuse. You are as guilty as the boy. Both of you are bad children." We were not lucky to be at the session when the court rendered the definitive judgment.

The end of school in December 1953 brought mixed feelings. It felt good to be out of school, but there was pain associated with the goodbyes to friendships we cherished and great anxiety over the pending results of the senior Cambridge school-certificate examinations we had just completed. We expected the results early in the following year. Anxiety was especially high because in many of the private schools, only a negligible few usually passed the examinations. Results were often not predictable. When they were finally released, only seventeen students out of the more than seventy who sat for the examinations passed. I was one of the lucky seventeen. It was joyful, and I could then look forward to a life of work.

Chapter 5

Early Working Life

Just four months after secondary school, I had a job. My excitement knew no bounds. Me, now a worker, earning regular monthly salary, and with my own home? Wow! It felt like wonderland. Having attained the senior Cambridge school certificate, I joined the Eastern Nigeria civil service. However, my ambition was also to improve myself academically. I had no intention of becoming a university teacher or a psychologist, my eventual careers. Instead, I set my eyes on the highest cadre of the civil service: the post of permanent secretary. In the 1950s, the permanent secretary position was most exalted and prestigious and one to which many bright young people aspired. A good number of bright clerical staff at the level of first-class clerk frequently got promoted to the permanent secretary position a few years after I joined the service. Immediately after secondary school, before the school certificate results were released, I had served as a teacher in a small school in Onitsha named Hope Rising Institute for three months, until April 1954. I joined the civil service on April 15, 1954. Because the family was in dire straits financially, I did not have the £1 sterling needed to register for the civil service entrance examination. Therefore, I had to settle for working as a clerical assistant for one year before I could advance to the regular post of third-class clerk.

It was a great time in the Nigerian civil service. There was order. Generally, staff did not malinger. Staff earned every penny they were paid by working seriously at their jobs. They appeared to enjoy their work and looked forward to being at work. Working overtime without seeking to be paid extra was normal, and no one complained. Supervisors were demanding. One of our supervisors was B. U. Usen. With him, you had to memorize the names of all the files in the department, hundreds and hundreds of them. If he called for a file and you seemed to be guessing, you were punished with a query. If he shouted "Piggery, Nkwelle Farm," you had better move straight to the dockets and produce the file, or else! There was real discipline and a strong work ethic.

Two years later, I was promoted to second-class clerk, after passing the promotion examination, which included typing, a skill that has been most helpful to me. (The personal computer later posed no difficulty for me since all I had to learn were the simple commands.) In 1959, I was transferred to Nekede Farm near Owerri after another promotion to the post of first-class clerk. Nekede Farm was interesting, and Owerri was a pleasant place to live in. The townspeople were warm and welcoming and non-natives were accorded all kinds of courtesies. Food was plentiful. I acted as the head clerk for a while, and my wife was headmistress of the primary school.

I had a small Sachs motorcycle and traveled the length and breadth of the area. My son Onyechi was born in Owerri. The one event that stuck in my mind was associated with the Epulemechi Society. In the Owerri Igbo dialect Epulemechi means, "how do I know I will be alive tomorrow?" The rule of the society was that each month, one individual would entertain the other members. On payday, he would bring his entire pay packet and use the money, down to the last penny, to entertain the group. (Pay days were regular and constant at that time.) The group's motto was that life was too short, and that entertaining oneself was proper since no one was certain of being around the next day. I tried that event once and opted out. I had so many responsibilities with my extended family, my mother, and siblings that being around tomorrow was not the issue. The question was whether I could harness my resources to deal with my numerous responsibilities.

From Nekede Farm, I was told to transfer back to Enugu. I was reluctant to abandon the comfort of Nekede Farm, the abundance of food and the hospitality of her people. People in Owerri, of which Nekede is a part, are joyful, and their hospitality is legendary. I went to Enugu to plead for a cancellation of the transfer. I met the chief clerk, Mr. Ihiekwe and pleaded, "Sir, kindly help me. I love working at Nekede Farm, and I am better able to manage my family responsibilities there, especially because the house rent is low compared to Enugu. The cost of living is less prohibitive."

With compassion in his voice, he said, "I know how you feel, young man, but the director of agriculture himself ordered this transfer." When I attempted to argue, he stopped me in my tracks and said, "Young man, you should be happy. The director examined the files of all the clerical staff and found you and another young man from the Port Harcourt office to be the best in the department. Therefore, he wants both of you to come and take charge of two sections, Stores and Personnel, at headquarters. This is recognition and possible promotion for you. Even your superiors are jealous."

After that, I realized that nothing I said would change things He advised me to pack my personal belongings and return to Enugu. I did just that, and this transfer gave me the opportunity to work and become friends with some very nice expatriates. E. W. Findlay, a Canadian, was a hard-working and decent gentleman. Some years later, in 1966, we exchanged views when I was in a student-exchange program at Michigan State University in East Lansing. The then deputy director of agriculture, a British man named David Jackson, and I shared many travel experiences on tours to Degema, Sagbama, Abonema, Yenagoa, Buguma, Oloibiri, Kolobiri, Brass, Port Harcourt, and other Nigerian towns, using the motor boat. David Jackson was a wonderful gentleman who appreciated nature and nature things. Although I was a lowly clerk, we found common ground in the appreciation of nature and in work. He asked me to call him by his first name and exhibited incredible warmth to me, though others found him somewhat reserved and distant. I did call him David when we were out of other people's hearing, but it was clear that he wanted that expression of familiarity even in the open.

The sights during those tours were glorious. We spent time in the motorized riverboat belonging to the department. Everyone would be on board, including the boat minders and cooks. We would be lulled to sleep by the waves gently swaying the boat. In the river towns, we woke up in the morning to wonderful sunrises, with the water birds flying around, signifying the beginning of a new day. The air was cool and refreshing and caressed the nostrils. After work, I would spend time watching beautiful birds and incredible multicolored sunsets over the waters, and also sharing poetry with others, mine as well as those from the classics. Unfortunately, during the Nigerian Civil War, I lost most of the photographic mementos of these joyful travels as well as other family memorabilia. David shared his successes with me, including the day he was awarded a master's degree by Cambridge University. Two years earlier, he had gone home and married his childhood sweetheart, a beautiful young lady, and brought her to Nigeria. He made a point of introducing me to her.

David and I shared so much laughter and fun. Sadly, laughter and fun went out of him when his beautiful wife died in Enugu during the birth of her first child. She was buried there. I don't know how well he handled that painful loss. He left for Britain soon afterward.

At Enugu, I was put in charge of the Stores section, a clearly challenging responsibility because the stores had the task of producing the animal feed for all the agricultural projects in Eastern Nigeria. That was the heyday of agriculture in Nigeria, when the premier of the Eastern region, Dr. Michael Iheonukara Okpara, championed agriculture in a way that had never happened before and, indeed, has never happened since. If that focus had continued in subsequent governments, Nigeria would have become the food basket of Africa. We had great, committed, young and dynamic officials, including such illustrious agriculturists like N. A. Nwosu and O. C. Menakaya. The main store was the Asata Mine Road store in Coal Camp, Enugu, where all the animal feed was processed. It was a rewarding work experience, and one felt great joy in being part of a promising evolving society. Work was enjoyable and fulfilling.

It was, as I mentioned earlier, a great time in the civil service, when commitment to excellence was the order of the day. One worked hard but did not seek to make gains beyond one's legitimate salary. For instance, delivery of grains was made to my stores in raffia bags while fishmeal and some other products were delivered in tins. These containers were disposable items, and no one seemed interested in what I did with them. Sometimes, as an incentive, I gave the bags to high-performing suppliers, who used them to re-supply grain. However, I saw that the sale of the used bags and tins would be an opportunity to enhance the department's income. I therefore arranged to sell these bags and tins and requested the headquarters accountant, a kinsman named John Iweanoge, to help me set up a process for documenting those sales. This activity brought substantial sums, thousands of pounds, into the government coffers. Today, such sales would go into private pockets, and I would be considered a moron for not appropriating those items. Indeed, my successor was quick to discard my fancy account books.

As is often the case with human beings, there were problems connected to relationships at work. I supervised about six young girls and four or five young men. Some of the young girls became the lovers of two or more of the senior staff, and it went to their heads. They would not work on their assignments. I queried them and that got me into trouble with one particular principal agricultural officer, who was quite high and powerful on the management team. Let us call him Mr. Ekong. Quite on the short side, he always seemed to want to be seen as powerful and to be noticed. A number of times, Mr. Ekong threatened to have me sacked or sent on transfer to Bamenda in the western Cameroon or to Yenagoa in Rivers Province. These were places that many staff members considered the equivalent of Siberia, well removed from the center of meaningful government activity. What he did not know was that as a riverine person, I was in love with the river, the ocean, and Yenagoa certainly would have been a good place for me. Furthermore, Bamenda was in western Cameroon, which was no longer part of Nigeria, but he still added it to the threat. The problem was that he never told me what my offense was!

I couldn't in good conscience stop pressuring the girls to do their work. Animal feed had to be prepared and dispatched promptly to the outstations, and monthly returns also had to be ready and on time. The statistics on which we based our stores operations (available inventories, projections, etc.) had to be up to date. And we had to worry about regular audit checks. So I reported the matter of the girls' intransigence to Mr. Findlay, who was in charge of my section. Ordinarily a soft-spoken man, in this instance, he reacted with unusual temper. He took up the matter with Mr. Ekong and the fellow left me alone to some degree, although he did not stop shouting at me and pointing threatening fingers at me from time to time.

In 1987, twenty-six years later, when I became a professor at the University of Lagos, a young girl with the same surname as my tormentor was assigned to me for supervision of her master's degree. One day, out of curiosity, I asked her, "Do you know Mr. Ekong who was an agricultural officer in Enugu?"

"Yes, I do, I do" she replied excitedly. "He is my father. I am his last child." Then I said to her, "Tell your father that Felix Uzoka, at one time an officer in charge of stores in the Ministry of Agriculture, is your teacher, your academic supervisor." She came back with the report that her father was excited by the information, saying that he and I were very good friends when we were in the Ministry of Agriculture and that he sent his warm greetings. I couldn't argue with that. The warm greetings were good enough for me. I made sure the young girl got the best supervision I could give. She was a very good student. I did not bother to tell her about my travails with her father.

Chapter 6

Woman

And the Lord God said, "It is not good that the man should be alone; I will make him an help meet for him."—Genesis 2:18

Woman, Nature's Magic
She is
My mother
My sister
My lover
My wife
My daughter
My woman, my woman
She is Nature's Magic

To Woman ...

My Way
If I had my way
And a goodly say
You won't lift a finger
Beyond the tender care you render
Nine months is work enough
In your world so ungodly rough
But that would be called chauvinism
By those who misconstrue feminism

To my dear mother, *Nwezekaibie*-Oyibonanu …

Endless Search
I tried Mama
I searched Mama
A good facsimile and
Nice Mama
But not the soup
Nor the care
Nor the glow
In my mama's eyes
Not the feel
Not as real
Nor yet the bond
Not as fond
Yes, Mama
A good facsimile
Yet Mama
Not my Mama.
So,
On bended knees,
Thank you, Mama.

To my sisters, Omebele Anne, Kate, Adaobi, Uzoamaka Stella …

The Foibles
Beloved mamas.
Adorable sisters
Our fond memories
Of shared affections
And warm stories
Of childhood foibles
Mitigating all worries
With strong adult caring
All because
You're my sisters

To my lover …

Alluring Fragrance
Sweet succulent essence
Entrancing presence
Let me take your nectar
And surrender
In the taking
My being
At your feet.

To my wife, SC …

Enduring Gift
A mother, a sister, a lover,
Rolled into one sweet flower,
Enduring gift
Without thrift
Of heaven's kindness
And I, a grateful witness.

To my daughters, Adaeze Susan and Ngozichukwu Lillian

Wonderland
Those sweet musings we shared
Unlimited endearments nurtured
The cooing and the giggles
And also the wiggles
Horse riding on my back
On all fours our meandering track
No pattern to draw
Crisscrossing the parlor floor
Amidst delightful shouts and joyous laughter
Unchained ardor, unfettered banter
And love eternally shared

To my fathers, my brothers, my sons and all the men in my life …

You all know.

Chapter 7

Getting Married

The year was 1956. It was three months short of my twenty-first birthday. I had finished secondary school in December 1953 and was working as a clerk in the Ministry of Agriculture at the Secretariat in Enugu. When I left school, I had rejected a couple of bank job offers because their working hours would not allow me to study, an ambition I'd nurtured early in life. I had a couple of girlfriends in the period following the end of secondary school and during my early employment. But given what I was earning then and my responsibilities to my family, marriage was certainly not on the agenda.

Why then would a twenty-one year old young man who had no resources to speak of, and whose friends were playing the field, get himself hooked up in marriage? When some of my friends heard that I was contemplating marriage, they thought I was crazy and said so to my face. "You mean you are going to leave all these beautiful girls and stick to one woman, at your age? You must be crazy!" That was the usual refrain from some friends, who kept lists of their conquests. I guess I was truly crazy, about Susan. You should have seen Susan and then gotten to know her; a beautiful and unusual person.

I was on my way home to Uwani, Enugu, coming up Zik Avenue from the Ogui Road area, approaching the Holy Rosary College on the hill. I had left work late after doing some overtime. After-work traffic was therefore minimal; only a few cars passed by. The foliage was lush and green, and a slight cool breeze signaled the approach of the Harmatan, the cold and windy dry spell. I was wearing the wide-bottomed shorts that were in vogue at the time; we called them boogie-woogie. My hair was parted on the left side, as it is even today, and I was full of self-confidence, rolling my blue, two-gear

Raleigh bicycle up the steep hill. I was feeling quite proud of myself. It was in this mood that I saw the unbelievable apparition of beautiful womanhood coming in my direction.

She came face to face with me. She was dressed in an enchanting wine-red dress that enhanced her graceful figure. She had a face to behold, radiant, with deep-set, mirthful eyes. Her complexion was an alluring sheen. Her gait was steady, measured, and firm, and she made no attempt at extra female flourish or posturing to emphasize her femininity. Later I wondered whether this was the result of years as a Girl Guide (equivalent to a Girl Scout). Yet her carriage, her allure, was enchantment in flesh. Perhaps Ryder Haggard imagined someone like her when he created the beautiful heroine in his epic novel *She*. I must have stared at her for eternity with my heart pounding inside me. I was speechless. I don't recall being affected by a woman like that before. Then it dawned on me that I had seen her before, briefly, in the company of my distant cousin Regina Ngoddy, her schoolmate. But out of school clothes, she certainly had become more like a woman, more elegant.

The connection to my cousin Regina gave me my opening. "Are you not Susan Borlin, Regina Ngoddy's friend?" I asked. Susan said, "Yes," with a puzzled expression on her face. I could see that she did not remember me right away.

"Do you live in Enugu?" I asked. Again, she replied, "Yes."

"And what are you doing in Enugu?"

"I am teaching at the Holy Rosary College, just up the hill," she said.

Then, with my heart pounding with hope, I asked the really important question, "Can I come visit you sometimes?" Her response was beyond my expectation. Susan said, "Yes, oh yes." The affirmation in her voice, perhaps exaggerated by me in that enchanting moment, kept me awake the whole night. I didn't waste any time before making my first visit. Those beautiful yeses led us to the altar and will now accompany both of us to eternity.

I was questioned by the Reverend Sisters in charge of Holy Rosary College, who were anxious to protect their teachers from the marauding young men. Usually, they did not allow male visitors in the premises. But the Reverend Sisters took a loving interest in me, and one of them, the Irish Reverend Sister Mary Ainia, even visited our home at Nsukka fifteen years later.

Oh, our courtship was a fantasy world, a world of dreams, both daydreams and night dreams. I would go to see her and she would walk me back to my place, and then I would walk her back to the school, and then again she would go back with me. Sometimes, we agreed to part in the middle of the road when it became difficult to stop going back and forth. We spent whole evenings walking and talking, oblivious of the dangers from the snakes in the grassy pathways we took. Many times we stopped to take in the moonlight and the stars, with endless hours of musings and heart-throbbing closeness. It wasn't about sex in the beginning. It was all in the heart and head, and we spent hours whispering sweet nothings that meant so much to us— about ourselves, our dreams, and our hopes. Although we were in the same town, less than a kilometer apart, we constantly sent love letters to each other; my sister Uzoamaka Stella was the dutiful courier.

Susan is four months younger than I am. I was born in July, while she was born in November of the same year. There was a tradition of women dating or marrying older men who had become established in their professions and could provide for them, but that did not seem to bother Susan or me. We were oblivious of the world around us. We had become, in a real sense, one.

When I went to Uncle Luke Chukwudebelu to announce my intended marriage, he was perturbed and said, "Are you now giving up education? How can you combine marriage and education? How are we to manage the school fees for the other family members ..." I told him I would continue with my education and that Susan and I had discussed how to accommodate our responsibilities to our families. (At that time, even he, the man who had raised me, was not yet married. He would marry a year or so later.)

My mother had a similar reaction. She said, "You are the *Diokpala,* the firstborn male. You are expected to help your siblings. What are the rest of the children to do if you get married so early and start a family? And also because you are similar ages, Susan, although pretty, is bound to look older than you very quickly." I told her I would continue to take care of my siblings and would address the matter of age (or looks) when the time came. For me, Susan would be ageless. I couldn't imagine her being old. Didn't my mother herself look young and beautiful?

Getting married to Susan was easier on my side of the family than it was on hers. At the time of our courtship, many men were asking for her hand in marriage the old-fashioned way. They were sending their relatives as emissaries to meet Susan's parents and to seek their consent. There was an engineer, a graduate teacher, a top civil servant, and many others. I took the direct approach. I asked Susan. Her mother was aghast. She could not understand why her daughter, her *Ada* (first daughter), would choose an urchin rather than one of the rich and established men who were actively courting her. "True," she said, "I know this young man comes from a well-known and respectable family, but what is he, himself?" In the Aboh (Ndokwa Igbo) dialect of Delta state, she asked her daughter, "Ife kena ka i funi i jeka nu?" (Is it this thing that you have found to marry?)

I was "this thing." My mother-in-law-to-be was unhappy, but we held our ground. She accepted the marriage grudgingly. And we were lucky. My father-in-law-to-be took to me immediately and liked me immensely. I could never figure out what he liked so much about the little urchin that was me.

The marriage process was truly traditional. Susan's hometown was Onya, located in the Ndokwa area of Delta State. But we share the same cultural heritage, with similar values and traditional practices, because her town is also part of the Ogbaru clan that stretches from Onitsha down both sides of the River Niger. They therefore treated me as they would their own kinsman. There was the initial "knocking on the door" (*i ku aka n'uzo*), when Uncle Luke and another relative took a bottle of gin to Susan's parents and informed them that "we are interested in something in your household." This was followed by a wine-carrying ceremony in which the drinks and other items were presented to Susan's extended family, with special items for her mother and father, including clothing items and a walking stick.

The actual traditional wedding began when Susan was given a cup (a small gourd) of palm wine by the head elder (*okpala*). She was asked to take a sip and present the drink to the man she had agreed to marry. After Susan had presented the drink to me, we were then asked to kneel before the elders for the special blessings and libations that would make us man and wife. After this, a team of six people, three members from each family, went into seclusion to negotiate the dowry. The outcome of the deliberations was not announced to the larger public but was told only to immediate family members. (In some neighboring Igbo groups, the dowry would have been negotiated and settled long before the traditional wedding ceremony, perhaps months earlier. However, people from Ogbaru prefer to do so during the traditional wedding ceremony itself. Some people make fun of this practice, saying that after the girl's family had been served alcoholic drinks, they would not be sober enough to ask for sufficient sums as dowry.)

My uncles and aunts on both sides of my family were all involved, and the traditional things were done to the last item. Besides the usual drinks and dowry, there were other requirements, such as that firewood would be fetched a certain number of times for the bride's family by the bridegroom. Usually, members of the bridegroom's family perform such tasks. I had an elderly uncle named Adizue who brought firewood to Susan's family on several occasions, carrying it on his head from the Obosi-Onitsha boundary to Susan's home in Fegge, a distance of several kilometers. He enjoyed participating in my wedding. Another townsman and also a good friend, Ambrose Chukwujindu, performed other tasks for Susan's family as demanded by tradition, including pounding yam into *foofoo* paste on several occasions. He enjoyed reminding Susan that he "married" her for me. It is easy to understand why my family members are able to call Susan *Nwunye-m* (my wife) or *Nwunye-anyi* (our wife) as is the tradition in Igbo land. It certainly makes sense. Family members often do more of the hard work in getting a wife into the family than the bridegroom does. In Igbo land, marriage is a family matter and not merely the business of the bride and bridegroom.

When we got married, my mother-in-law kept her distance, but I did not let her be. I would travel to Onitsha on some weekends and stay with her in her market stall. She sold dried fish brought down from the north. She was a big-time fish trader. She found me troublesome. I made a nuisance of myself around her. If she left the stall, I sold her fish as I deemed fit or as I thought was the right price. She would scream, "This boy is about to ruin me!" When I got hungry, I would ask her to order food for both of us, and we ate together. Initially, she would not introduce me to her business colleagues. I believe she was ashamed of introducing this little urchin as her daughter's husband. But I quickly got the better of her. As time passed, she even began to miss me if I did not show up.

Gradually, she came around and practically adopted me as her first son. If she had a disagreement with her husband, even on sexual matters, she would send for me. If she wanted to give loans to fishermen on the annual fishing trip to the north, she would ask me to help prepare the agreements. She enjoyed giving these loans, most of which were never repaid. A few people paid the paltry interest, but not the principal. Others merely brought token gifts of fish in appreciation for the loan. In fact, some people took new loans even when they had not paid back the old ones. It was obvious to me that she just enjoyed the status symbol of being able to give loans and the accompanying homage paid to her. It did not matter whether or not people actually paid back the loans. She was so good-natured about it and bore no ill will. In fact, it surprised me that she sometimes made excuses on behalf of her debtors. "Wa afuna li" (they can't even feed themselves), she would often say in her Aboh Igbo dialect.

In the end, we became good friends, and reportedly on her deathbed, she bemoaned the fact that she would not see her favorite son-in-law before her death. (We were then in the United States of America.) I too became very fond of her. She was a great lady, and I never held it against her because she wished for the best husband for her daughter. Isn't that what I also wished for my own daughters? At the time of my wedding, I was clearly ineligible as a suitor, that is, in the estimation of society, particularly since Susan, with her high elementary teacher's certificate, was in the top class of educated women in Nigeria. And she was beautiful. With only a secondary school certificate and a clerical job, I certainly seemed dwarfed by the car-owning suitors. I can't explain it, but the status factor did not bother me; I felt fully confident in myself. I often tease Susan now. I tell her that if she had not married me, she would have been a widow twenty years ago, when the last of her then "eligible" suitors passed away.

Why did I get married so early? One reason is that I was not really good at playing the field. The real reason, of course, was Susan. Although I did not have much experience with women or girls, Susan was unique. She exuded beauty in a calm and un-intimidating manner. Who said the beautiful ones were not yet born? Aside from her enchanting visage, she had so much humility. She was gentle and genteel. She carried herself with dignity and without arrogance. She was loving, caring, and giving. She cared about her family deeply. She cared about her faith. Her cooking was second only to my mom's. And, more than anything, she loved me. For me, that was one love I could not let go. She was the dream of any man who wanted to settle down, so I settled for her. I am eternally glad I did so. She has made living worthwhile.

Our first baby, Adaeze Susan, came on July 20, 1957, a year after our marriage in 1956 and three days before my twenty-second birthday. How can I describe the joy of cuddling that sweet little girl in my arms, all mine? I was delirious with joy. But I was awkward with the baby, thinking she would break or fall apart if I held her the wrong way. I am still uneasy with little babies. They seem so fragile and vulnerable. However, that day remains one of the happiest in my life. Oh, there was immeasurable joy with all the children and the grandchildren, beginning with Uche Ngoddy, our first grandchild, but that first experience was all consuming

However, in marriage I had a whole lot of growing up to do. (Does anyone actually stop growing up and learning at any age? When I was seventy, my grandson Kadizue, aged seventeen and just finishing his secondary-school education, took me to a cybercafé and taught me how to operate my own e-mail.) Remember, I was barely twenty-one, just entering adulthood when I got married. Why don't they teach people about marriage and being a family man or woman? In the beginning phase of marriage, there were family boundaries to negotiate and define. There were rights, privileges, and duties to define—between Susan and myself and between us and our two families. We did pretty well in this by achieving necessary independence while retaining and nurturing the loyalty and support systems that surrounded us.

On reflection, however, I am often amused at some of my antics. For example, being nurtured in the traditional life style, I imagine that, unconsciously, I held the misguided notion that a real man demonstrates his authority firmly by showing the world that he is in charge. One result was that I found myself asking Susan to fetch water for me each time there was a visitor in the house. That way, our visitors would clearly see that I was truly in charge, that I was a real man. For a while, I was not conscious of this aberration, and I must have been drowning myself in water that I did not need.

After several months of this puerile routine, I had something of an awakening. I sat up one evening and asked myself, "Why do I have to prove anything to anybody? Do I have to prove to anyone that I am a man when I was man enough to marry a wife?" The next day, when a visitor arrived, I asked Susan whether *she* needed a drink. Used to the routine, she got up to fetch the drink, but I restrained her gently with my hand and told her to sit down. I went into the room and brought water for myself and for her and served her in the presence of the visitor. That was *uhuru*, my *uhuru*, my emancipation. Thank God that the notion of the man getting back from work and propping up his feet and reading his newspapers and being ministered to, was not part of my upbringing in the work, work, and more work ethic of the Nwachie household.

There were other interesting events. I love cooking. I pride myself on being a good cook. Having performed all household chores when I lived with the Nwachies, while staying with my uncle, and also in my brief bachelor life, I actually began to miss cooking. One day, my mother-in-law found me in the kitchen cooking, something I still do now and again. She was aghast. She asked me what I was doing in her daughter's kitchen. (Her daughter's kitchen? The kitchen that was mine a few months earlier had become her daughter's kitchen? Yet her daughter wasn't paying the rent!) In a clearly anguished voice, she asked, "Ya bu ife opusani bu shi azunam Suzy nwam azu, shi o shipu ite nke oma?" (Are you insinuating that Suzy, my daughter, was not properly brought up by me, that she cannot cook well?)

"Not so, Mama, not so." I said to her. "Susan's cooking is great, only next to my mom's. I just enjoy cooking sometimes." It took some time for her to accept this unmanly excuse if, in fact, she truly ever did. I even joked with her that the cooks who worked for the white men on river boats were men, not women. But she countered by saying that those men did not cook in their own homes with their wives watching. I had to fight to regain my right to cook, even to wash my own clothes if I felt like doing so. Did I get married to lose the freedom to perform the tasks I enjoy doing? For me, this realization was *uhuru*, real freedom, real growing up, and real manhood. We made sure that our children, boys and girls, all learned to cook and do their family chores.

Over a full lifetime, as we move into our seventies and celebrate almost fifty years of marriage, Susan and I have shared a philosophy of life that has seen us through thick and thin. When things get really rough and tough, Susan would say, "Az, this too will pass." And indeed, whatever it was would pass, leaving us stronger for the experience. Did we have any disagreements? Of course we did and still do; in fact, our children say we are always arguing.

But we never had any deep-set or lasting disagreements. We certainly do not take disagreements to bed. The distressed couples I counsel in marital therapy often laugh when I tell the men who allow their quarrels to last beyond the day that they are losing out at night on the dowry they paid, not to mention all the hassles they went through in marrying their wives. Or I get a knowing look or nod from one or the other spouse when I suggest that a continuing quarrel is one partner's ploy of keeping a disagreement alive to avoid performing his or her conjugal duties. Marital peace and harmony impose on each spouse the obligation to accept and give affection.

Susan and I have graduated from calling ourselves pet names, Maxi (me) and Wini (her), to calling each other Az (me) and SC (her). Now we join the children, grandchildren, and other family members in calling ourselves Papa and Mama, to the amusement of many visitors who overhear us. We have a whistle sound to call each other when we are some distance apart, whether at home or in a crowd. Being married to Susan felt good more than fifty years ago, and it feels good now. She says it feels good to her too.

Chapter 8

Coping with Death

What is it about death that consumes us? Perhaps it is due to the phenomenon of non-being, of irrevocable separation, and eternal distance? I have had my share, including the death of my first son, Uchenna Felix. A handsome and intelligent boy, Uchenna Felix was adored by everyone, especially my mother. He was her first grandson, and she fussed over him. She, in fact, was the one who named him Uchenna (God's will). He was also popular in our entire neighborhood around Zik Avenue. A barber worked in one of the shops on the ground floor of our apartment building, and often Uchenna would spend time with him talking like some grown up. He was only four years old. When Uchenna died, the barber quickly packed up and left, saying he couldn't work in that shop without thinking of the boy.

Uchenna's death resulted from a home accident. A servant was boiling water, and by accident the kettle fell off the stove, and Uchenna was scalded. We went to the hospital, where a number of the doctors were my friends. He improved rapidly. On the day before he was to be discharged, I paid for a goat to celebrate. But in the evening he began to have seizures and fits. He had tetanus. I overheard the doctors asking themselves, "Did we give him ATS?"—that is, an anti-tetanus serum. It turned out they had not. At that time, I did not have enough medical awareness to insist on such precautionary medical steps as I now do. Within an hour, Uchenna died. Now, the story is about my grieving and an old gravedigger.

The next morning, on the day he was to be buried, I was the first to arrive at the mortuary. The mortuary was bare and badly kept; a drab, empty room with cracks all over the floor. Bodies were just thrown about. It was not a place for my son, I moaned inwardly. Modern facilities have made mortuaries somewhat more decent and dignified places for the dead.

In my grief and in tears, I held my son's body up, shaking him, hoping that he would come alive. Death didn't seem real. At that moment, a family friend, Nelson Moore who worked with the Public Works Department, came in, hit me rather savagely on my back, and told me to get out of the morgue. "Are you the only one who has ever lost a child" he asked, rather unsympathetically, I thought. Looking at me straight in the eyes, he continued, "You behave as if you are the only one who had ever lost a child. You act as if you own the children. Don't you know that God owns all children and takes them back when he pleases?"

In my grief, Nelson Moore's logic was lost on me. I had difficulty comprehending a God who would give such great joy as children and then on a whim, takes them back, just like that! I was twenty-seven years old, with a great attachment to my first son. Losing him seemed like the end of the world. I could not honestly comprehend God's disposition on death, and I must have blasphemed sufficiently during that period to be damned. I grieved for a long time, and I would go to the graveyard on my Honda Benley motorcycle, sit on the mound that marked his grave, and cry, pray, and quarrel with the Creator, before heading to work. I repeated the same routine on my way home. I continued this ritual for some time.

On one of my trips to the graveyard late one afternoon, a wizened old man, the supervisor of the team working there, beckoned to me. He told me to follow him. He started walking through freshly dug and filled graves in the children's section. Seeing that I was hesitant, he urged me to follow his footsteps. In Nigeria at that time, before the civil war, people had considerable fear of and reverence for graves. That was my frame of mind. Graves were not places on which you stepped. But seeing that the old man was serious, I obeyed him, uncomfortable as I was. Something about the old man seemed compelling. He asked me questions about my son, including his age, whether he was in preschool, etc., perhaps to hold my attention. At the end of a long row of graves, he turned around and began walking back on another row of graves to the place at which we'd started. I followed him, but with increasing discomfort.

When we finally stopped, he asked me to point out where my boy's grave was. I did, pointing at a plot of land some considerable distance from the new graves. Many more children had been buried since my son Uchenna. Then the old man looked at me and asked, "Do you know what is inside the mounds we have just walked on?"

I said, "Children. Dead children." He told me to look again at the mounds we had just walked on and asked, "Do you know that these children under the ground have parents?" I said, "Yes."

Then he said, "Look around again. Do you see any of their parents here wailing and crying?" I said "No."

He said, "Do you have any other child?" I said "yes."

Then he asked, "Do you know that there are couples who do not have one child, never had one?" I said "Yes."

After a short pause, he delivered what I believe was the intended blow: "Young man, the day you grow up, when you become a man, like the other parents whose children lie here, you will not waste your time here, but go home and take care of the other children God gave you."

I was taken aback by the old man's comment. It contained the grains of sympathy but only if one was reflective enough, which I was not at that moment. I felt only veiled reproach. Yet, his manner and his tone were warm. I thanked him, went away, and never went to the graveyard again. Whether this was due to fear of meeting the old man again, the shame of being chided for not being grownup, or his advice that I should look after my other children, I will never know. The first sounds like the most plausible motive. I never went to the graveyard again. Perhaps his gentle admonition helped me to cope with Uchenna's death and the subsequent death of my youngest son, Arinzechukwu, from leukemia, a harrowing experience for us and for him.

Does any death ever prepare anyone for the others that follow? Somebody once said something about the death of a child being a permanent sore, an unending grief for the parents. Indeed, can death ever be forgotten? The birthdays, the shared joys from the cradle, the innocence of mind and spirit, the individual disposition of each child—these are enduring images. Memory keeps the dead alive, but we always have to make a choice about whether to remember pleasant or unpleasant attributes. Perhaps, real healing is in the celebration of the gift of a child's presence in one's life; the enhancing of memory with the joyful events; the laughter, the fun, the child's special quirks, and so on. The answer, it seems, is to dwell on the shared moments of love and communion rather than on the loss itself, to be always thankful that a particular child touched one's life, no matter how brief.

I am not sure, however, that my early experiences with death (my father, my son) truly prepared me for other losses, especially the deaths of Uncle Luke Chukwudebelu and my mother. Uncle Luke died in 1971 while I was in the United States. He and I had forged a bond well beyond the ordinary. He had become a father. In addition, beyond the family responsibilities we shared, we also shared confidences and had a truly close relationship. We were friends. Some weekends, if I went to Onitsha, I would get his clothes ready for Sunday mass and, on occasion, he would ask me to cook some special soup he liked. This was after we both were married. I enjoyed doing that for him, and we would eat together. His wife made light of this, but would wonder whether this meant something was lacking in her cooking. Nonetheless, she ate the meals with us. There was no way she could do otherwise, seeing the bond between her husband and me.

In 1971, I was in a doctoral program in Miami, Florida, and working on a student assignment with the African Studies Center, whose director was Tom Uguru. Susan and the children were still in Nigeria. One morning, I saw a letter in Susan's handwriting addressed to Mr. Uguru. I was puzzled. Susan did not know him, although I had informed her that he was the director of the unit where I was working. There was no reason for Susan to write to him. Meanwhile, he was away on a month-long tour. Not being able to contain my curiosity over the reason for the letter, I called him and told him about the letter. He too was puzzled and was also anxious to know why Susan had written to him. He told me to open the letter and read it to him. It was a plea to Mr. Uguru to find a humane way of breaking the news of Uncle Luke's death to me and helping me cope with the loss. Uncle Luke had died suddenly from a heart attack right after a meal.

I was devastated. My siblings and I called him Papa, not Uncle. That was not just in line with tradition. He had truly become a caring father. He had love in his heart for everyone, inside and outside the family, and an immensely generous disposition. To this day, he remains an example of human kindness among the people in my town. Once, some people who were associated with the family through the unfortunate legacy of slavery, requested land for building a house. However, the available land had been designated as ancestral land. There was intense objection to the request because the people were descendants of slaves and under the prevailing culture should not be accorded such privilege. Uncle Luke's reaction was violent. I'd never seen him disagree with his relatives and other elders so violently before. He shouted at them in Igbo, "Unu cholu ka fa bili na ikuku?" (Do you want them to live in the air?) He had his way, and the people got the land. Uncle Luke's death was the death of our father happening all over again. Another loss, another beginning. And this thrust me toward the apex of family leadership, a daunting task. I was in mourning for a long time, and my schoolwork suffered. I had to snap out of it somehow, being alone in America without easy communication with my family. I mourned alone.

The next death we faced was that of our youngest child and son, Arinzechukwu Stanley. That was in 1976. We were in Miami, Florida. Susan was working on her master's degree in early childhood education, and I was working on my doctorate degree. After suffering from an ordinary fever that we thought would go away, Arinzechukwu was diagnosed with having acute lymphocytic leukemia. We were stunned. The diagnosis of leukemia was a sentence of imminent death. There was no known cure for leukemia, especially the acute form of the disease. We were suspicious of the diagnosis. We sought other explanations; perhaps it was malaria, which American doctors often did not consider when making their primary diagnoses. After consulting a number of Nigerian doctors in Miami, however, we finally did accept it.

Well, not quite. To this day, I have remained unconvinced about the diagnosis. So much has been written about how certain human populations are used for experimental research into diseases that one is obliged to be skeptical about diagnoses. Was my son a victim of such an evil act? The search for leukemia treatment continues still, so who knows? Indeed, we may never know. As I write this, thirty years after my son's death, five Bulgarian nurses and a Palestinian doctor have been found guilty of deliberately infecting young healthy Libyan children with the HIV/AIDS virus, reportedly to find a cure for the disease. Fifty of the unfortunate children had died at the time of court proceedings. The court in Libya sentenced the doctor and nurses to death, and there was intense diplomatic lobbying around the matter, urging a fresh trial. There were those who questioned the legal proceedings, because they believed that the charges were politically motivated. In a fresh trial, the verdict was again "guilty." This is certainly not an isolated event in medical history and US medical history has its own examples, such as the Tuskegee experiment on syphilis in which only blacks (399 black men) were used as the study subjects and unfortunate victims of medical inhumanity. The unfortunate subjects were denied the available treatment for syphilis, in order to determine the natural progression of untreated syphilis. Human evil is alive and well. Anyway, at the time of Arinzechukwu's illness, our options were limited.

We suffered through about eleven months—contemplating death during an extremely harrowing treatment regimen. It was before the current options of bone marrow transplants, newer medicines, and gene therapy, and the treatment for the condition was worse than the disease. The drugs damaged more than they healed. They were all experimental drugs, some with undetermined and dangerous side effects, including severe organ damage. I am not sure that things have changed much since then.

The oncology ward was a most depressing place, with children counting the number of their fellow patients who had died and who was likely to die next. No day would pass without one or two young people dying in the ward. Arinzechukwu was a brave little boy. He was quite mature for his age, counting the days to his eight birthday party at the time of the diagnosis. He sometimes babysat children older than himself. Parents, white and black, were happy to leave their children in his care. Even in sickness, Arinzechukwu was heroic and encouraged us greatly. He would urge his mother to go to her class even if he was in pain. He would get up in the morning and fry an egg for himself in the hospital kitchen. He once offered breakfast to his doctor, who was delighted, expressing surprise and delight at the young man's independence. Arinzechukwu sometimes walked over to other children in the ward and encouraged them to bear their pain and take their medications. He turned himself into a social worker on the ward.

On the day he died, he was aware he was dying. He said to us, "My legs are cold. I am having no feelings there. That's what happened when others died." The hospital ward was an open affair, and some nurses indiscreetly discussed cases in the presence of the patients. Perhaps because the patients were mostly children, hospital personnel assumed they did not understand what was being said. Susan, feeling much anguish, started to leave Arinzechukwu's side, but I persuaded her to stay. We both stayed with him. The last thing he said to us was comforting and heartrending: "You know, if I come to this world again, I want you to be my parents. You are wonderful parents, wonderful Mommy and Daddy."

Almost in unison Susan and I said, "Ari, you are a wonderful son and we are lucky to have you. You are a special gift from God."

Even as I write this, I still feel the impact of that final statement; such depth of affection from a seven-year-old boy. Arinzechukwu was such a caring, loving person, and his loving spirit was captured in that statement. We kept talking to him with familiar endearments, massaging his dying legs and arms. He kept moving his head when his name was called, until he passed away. We stayed by his bedside for about an hour when the nurses came to take his body away. We cried, holding hands. The pain was harsh. We had no family nearby to console us. And we had the additional anguish of having to tell the other children that their brother was no more.

Arinzechukwu was a favorite of my mother, who wanted us to bring his body home to her. The airlines said we had to provide a hermetically sealed coffin to transport the body from Miami to Nigeria. One month afterward, I took him home to his grandma and the family. My brother Okwudili met us at the airport in Lagos, and we drove to Onitsha. The body kept well. The undertaker's magic was evident. He didn't look dead, especially with a cap covering his head, which had lost all its hair due to the awful cancer medications. Mom insisted that she had to spend a day with him. We kept the coffin open, and Mom stayed with him until the next morning when we took him to our village, Atani, and buried him in our ancestral home. After the burial, Mom said, "Arinzechukwu nwam a nata go." (Arinzechukwu my child has come home.)

My mother died of uterine cancer in 1986, ten years after Arinzechukwu's death. I had quite a few experiences with her illness and death that were touching. I was away on a research trip to Kenya and Zambia, I believe, when she took ill. My brother Okwudili took her to a well-known gynecologist who was an associate professor of medicine at one of the older universities in the country. The doctor did the initial diagnosis, which he said was tentative. But I knew the danger signs. When I asked my mother what the problem was, she said, "I suddenly started to have my menses again."

Since she was over sixty and had been menopausal, I knew there was danger. The immediate problem, however, was that my mother was not happy with the doctor. Her complaint? The doctor was too young! For people of my mother's generation, sexuality was a very sensitive matter. She was emotionally distraught at the thought of the youthful-looking doctor "fiddling" with her during the medical examination. The doctor had a slight build, which might have made him look younger than he was since he could not be that young and attain his level of achievement in the academic world. My mother's perception of his age, however, was a mark against the highly qualified doctor. (Incidentally, I met the good doctor at a social function about twenty years later, and he still looked quite youthful and sprightly, with only a few strands of white hair. Mom would have had the same complaint still.)

I understood my mother's predicament and we agreed to find another doctor. We decided to move her to the University of Nigeria Teaching Hospital in Enugu, first ensuring that she could see a seasoned elderly doctor who was also competent and reputable. Luckily, we found one. Dr. Uche was a well-known and respected gynecologist who was also elderly, portly, with a magnificent shock of white hair. Mom's reaction was predictable. She said, "Ehe! Nka bu ezigbo doctor." (Oh, yes! This is a proper doctor.)

Dr. Uche and my mother hit it off very well. He was a very good person and a humane, old-fashioned physician, who paid attention to his patients beyond the call of duty. The hospital was his life. The women took to him very easily. Another advantage was that our dear friends, Professor Amankulor and his wife, were family friends of the doctor. Regina Amankulor, a well-trained nurse, was especially helpful to us. Mom comfortable, but her condition was bad. The doctor recommended surgery.

On the appointed date, we all gathered at the hospital. While she was being wheeled into the surgery, she asked the aides to stop. She beckoned to me and said, "Just in case I don't make it, remember to be patient with your brothers and sisters and other relatives. I know you are. Nevertheless, you will be angered now and then, but remember you are a leader and a leader is patient. Some of them can be particularly difficult, but you already know that. So, be patient over any provocation."

I reassured her, saying, "Don't worry Ma. You know I will be patient.

Haven't I always been patient? Go on Ma, stop worrying." Comforted, she then went into surgery.

After a short while, the doctor still wearing his surgical gown and cap, came out and called Mrs. Amankulor and my wife Susan aside. He told them something; later I learned that he asked them whether I could "take" the kind of news he had for me. Their answer was yes. Dr. Uche then called me over and said, "Dr. Uzoka, I will put things bluntly. Your mother's condition is bad. The cancer has spread. In our medical lingo, it has metastasized. If I operate and make all the excisions, your mother might not leave the theater alive. If I close up without touching anything, you may have up to two months to prepare for her death." Without hesitation, I said, "Doctor, just close up."

When my mother came to after the surgery, she asked me how things were. I was obliged to lie to my mother for the first time in my adult life. I said, "Fine, very fine. You're fine, Mama. It all went well."

I cannot fully explain the pain caused by that lie, necessary as it might have been. The anguish I felt was palpable. My mother continued her post-surgery recovery in the hospital and was discharged after a while; I imagine when the surgical wound had healed some. At some point, home care became very difficult due to the clearly unbearable pain, and we were again obliged to hospitalize her in Enugu. The cancer ward is the most depressing place on Earth, with its sense of finality; the anguished pain of the patients; the unceasing moaning and sometimes curses directed at someone, the gods, or to God; and the inevitable grieving of family and friends, well ahead of death, all signifying the mood of the final days. Many patients also lost their self-esteem because of the absence of privacy, exemplified by occasional stark nakedness, on the ward. Indeed, too many patients lost interest in protecting their physical privacy. One felt a sense of "what's the point" in their attitude.

A number of incidents touched me deeply during my mother's last stay in hospital. Mother had had an earlier disagreement with my sister Adaobi, the child of my father's third wife. Her mother left shortly after her birth, and my mother raised her. She was introduced to her natural mother years later when she was more than ten years old. Adaobi and my mother were very close. However, in the past few years, they had grown apart. One reason was that Adaobi had turned away from her biological mother following a bitter dispute. My mother tried to intervene and Adaobi felt that she was taking sides with her biological mother and that brought the two of them into conflict.

In the hospital, my mother lamented that she was about to die without resolving things with Adaobi. I went to Asaba in Delta State, where Adaobi resided, and told her what was going on. She was visibly troubled and rushed to Enugu, abandoning her business. The sight of the two of them during their initial meeting brought tears to my eyes. They hugged and cried together, voiced their pains, and made up. Adaobi was at mother's bedside when she passed away. Mother died in her arms. In my clinical practice, I have found that there is so much emotional healing for the dying when disordered human relationships are resolved. Living relatives and friends are also better able to cope with the mourning process.

Another incident was my encounter with one of the nurses in the ward. My mother was in agony. Ordinarily a stoic person, she could not hide her distress, and in one of her few moments of respite, she would say in jest that the pain was worse than that of childbirth because it was unceasing and had no foreseeable pleasant ending. I do not know if anything equals the pain that accompanies cancer. She was constantly moaning as were the other patients, except those that had just been given what one of the doctors called Brompton's cocktail, a sedative (laced with narcotics) that was usually given to terminal patients to alleviate unbearable and intractable pain. I imagine that the nurse, seeing our anguish and assuming I was the oldest and presumably responsible for Mom's care, took me aside and said, "I see your mother is suffering. Is it not better to help her to get on, to end this suffering, instead of forcing her to endure all this pain with no possibility of recovery?"

I understood what she meant: euthanasia. I thanked her for her concern but said that I could not in any way shorten my mother's life. I saw the compassion in her face and felt it in her voice, but I could not bring myself to do it. I told her that I hoped to find such a compassionate nurse by my bedside at my own end, in case I sought such assistance. At some point, she became worried that I would report her to a higher authority but I reassured her that I appreciated her deep concern, and my family became friends with her.

Euthanasia was certainly an option, but not with someone else's life and most certainly not with my mother's life, not with the womb that bore me. And even with my own life, would I want God's wrath with me for ending what I did not start? Yet, one has to acknowledge the deep emotions and empathy that propel nursing and medical staff to suggest or implement such an option. Or indeed the anguish and pain, both physical and emotional, that compel people to seek this final resolution of their anguish.

There was one other notable transaction with mother in her final days. I visited the hospital every day during her stay. Between lecture periods and clinic engagements, I would drive the seventy kilometers from Nsukka, the university town where we lived, to spend time with her and also to find out if there were new treatment regimes that required my attention or money. A few days before she passed on, she called me to her side and said, "Azubikem, you come here every day from Nsukka. I think you should rest and not come every day. Suppose something happens to you on these daily drives? They will say that I have used my son to save my life through witchcraft."

That was just like Mom. Even in her distress, she worried about me. She insisted, but the next day, I did not comply with her wishes. I don't now recall, but I believe there was some compelling reason for me to go to Enugu besides the desire to see her every day. I drove there in the company of my lifelong friend, Dr. Hyacinth Obi-Keguna. We parked my Peugeot 504 saloon car by the water tank behind the Ward 12. Mom was visibly upset with me and did not accept my excuses for coming to Enugu. When Hyacinth and I got back to the car, we found that the propeller shaft had fallen out of its connection and onto the ground, even though we had driven to the hospital, more than seventy kilometers, without any problems. It was a truly unbelievable and, according to our mechanics, unusual event. We could do nothing about it so we locked the car and took public transportation back to Nsukka.

The next morning, I sent my mechanic, Goddy Achiakpa (nicknamed Bekee because his skin color is very pale) to the hospital to repair and retrieve the car. On that morning, I obeyed Mom's order and did not go to Enugu to see her. She died the morning of the following day just before I arrived at the hospital. She was clutching her rosary beads. Her faith was strong. She had been baptized Mary several years back, with our family friend Theresa Iweanoge serving as her godmother. She looked so peaceful in death. Her face was relaxed, not drawn anymore. Calmness had overtaken all physical struggles. Even with the unbearable grief, I was consoled by her escape from anguish. Mom was finally at peace.

Mom's death brought us face to face with custom and tradition. At the time of her death, two of her younger brothers were still alive and, indeed, one of them, John Uzowulu, had participated actively in decisions regarding her treatment and stayed with us when Mom was discharged from the hospital after her surgery. In Igbo culture, especially in my own subculture, the burial of one's father, brothers, and unmarried sisters often takes place without a hitch. You practically can do with them whatever you wish. But the burial of a mother is another matter altogether. You dare not bury your mother without the permission of her ancestral family. Indeed, in some stricter towns, a mother's body is routinely taken back to the ancestral home for burial. No request to bury her elsewhere is entertained; there is no negotiation on the matter at all. In my culture, the proceedings in these consultations often are characterized by strong emotions on the part of the deceased's ancestral family and occasionally become truly arcane transactions.

Tradition demanded that upon mother's death we had to inform her family three times of the event. Some families could insist that this information should be delivered on three separate days, but in most cases the three visits to the deceased's ancestral home would be on the same day and sometimes a few minutes apart. First we had to tell the elders, who had assembled in a hurry and now were seated and waiting, that "Our mother is sick." We presented to them a bottle of gin and some kola nuts. The family told us to take good care of her and take her to a good doctor; they didn't want anything to happen to their beloved daughter.

On the second visit a few minutes later, we informed the family that Mom was in bad shape; in fact, she was very ill and was not responding to treatment. They urged us again to take good care of her and make sure that nothing happened to her. Even my maternal uncle, John Uzowulu, who was with us for most of the period of her ill health and helped take Mom's body to the mortuary, vehemently urged us to make sure that their precious daughter did not die. Finally, we went in, again with drinks and kola nuts, to say that our mother had died. Anger and shouts broke out, suggesting that we might not have cared for her enough and instructing that we bring their daughter's body home to them promptly. The daughters of the family lineage, married and unmarried, (called the *umu-ada*) were the most vociferous, shouting and threatening hell and brimstone if we failed to comply.

Negotiations about Mom's burial then began in earnest. We pleaded with them to allow us (*Umu-nwadiani*, their nephews and nieces) to have the privilege of burying our mother in her marital home: "We would be on your side now, if Mother was born a man and had us children. We are your children too." Long and heated arguments about whether we deserved the privilege followed. The chief elder (*okei*) asked, "Did they look after our sister well while she lived? Did they show sufficient interest in her ancestral home? Are they good *umu-nwadiani*, good nephews and nieces?" They also wanted to know where we would bury mother. Was the intended burial place respectful of her distinguished lineage and family background? There were jokes from some of my friends in Mom's lineage, who said to me in Igbo, "Cholum ife ka'm welu kwado yi." (Find something for me, a tip, so that I will lend you my support.) I abused them in jest. They didn't mean any harm, of course. Such exchanges are part of the drama of funeral customs in a situation where there had been goodwill and also warm relations prior to the death.

After several rounds of consultations among Mom's people, they called us in to announce that they were granting us the privilege of burying our mother in her marital home. We were good children, good *umu-nwadiani*, they said, who had given their daughter proper attention in life and there was no reason for them to deny us continuing communion with her in death. One of the elders recalled my brother Okwudili's action over our mom's access to fish. Okwudili did not want Mom to bother with fish costs, so he made arrangements with the fish sellers in our town, who let her take any fish that she wanted, fresh or dried without asking her for money. I believe he made deposits to cover any possible purchase. The elders all echoed their satisfaction that Mom was well cared for in life. We thanked them profusely for their kind disposition to us and assured them that they would participate in Mother's funeral and that we would continue our relationship with them in the years ahead. We didn't intend to sever links with them because Mom had died. We also assured them that all their traditional entitlements (including a cow and a goat) would be promptly delivered to them. They were pleased. Mom's funeral was wonderful, with the participation of the church and all relevant groups and the full involvement of her ancestral family.

One of the wonderful aspects of Mom's funeral was the array of people who came forward to publicly state that Mom had either paid school fees for their children or their rent now and again for them. I could not believe my ears. Mom had no income of her own and depended on us children to take care of her, yet she saved something out of what we gave her to engage in charity work. It was so heartwarming and a continuing lesson from the grave for her children.

She played mother to both young and old in her neighborhood and well beyond. The children's block rosary prayer group for the neighborhood was held in front of her residence. When we tried to relocate her to a more comfortable accommodation, she flatly refused, saying that she would not leave her "children." In addition, the church was only a five-minute walk away. She often attended morning mass, escorted by her pet dog. Many of the young people in the neighborhood got to know us and in later years would walk up to me in recognition, saying, "I know you. Are you not Mama's son?"

More than this, Mom was the neighborhood counselor. People with personal and marital problems went to her for advice. Soft-spoken and on the quiet side, Mom was a bundle of wisdom, with unceasing empathy for people. I recall one such case. A young woman went to Mom in tears over her husband's behavior, especially his philandering and frequent absences from home. They had frequent fights. I do not recall the full details, but as the lady often tells me, Mom gave her a recipe for dealing with her husband that sounds very much like a classic behavior-modification procedure. Instead of bickering with her husband, she was to ignore him. It worked. The lady continues to credit the long-term success of her marriage to Mom's intervention. Mom's wisdom and wise counsel also saw me through quite a number of tight spots. Now and again, I wonder if I would not have done much better if I had stayed with Mom, instead of spending over a decade in school with all the hassles, anxiety-ridden examinations, associated with learning how to become a psychologist and how to change behavior!

There were other deaths, other passings. My father-in-law and mother-in-law died while I was in the United States. They were both buried in their ancestral home in Onya, Delta State. I grieved for the good parents they were to me. Then my sister Anne died when she was planning a trip to see me. She was a diabetic. The family was hurt. Anne was a loving person. We buried her in our ancestral home. Her daughter Ayo, a wonderful human being and beloved by all, died soon after, following childbirth. Again, the family was in mourning for a dear child of the family. Ayo's husband, Laide Adelami, a warm and terrific human being took the loss real hard.

Thoughts about death can be disconcerting. I recall the passing of a dear friend and colleague, Chris Onyedike, who worked at the University of Lagos in the Department of Estate Management. We would spend time arguing all day about one event or the other. Chris was such a delightful person. He would ask Susan to prepare fresh fish pepper soup with a great deal of pepper in it, like some Spanish chili sauce. In fact, he would be fanning his tongue while clearly enjoying the soup! I refused to eat it with him. My palate couldn't take that much pepper. In addition to his vast knowledge in his field, Chris was one human being I found to be completely knowledgeable in practically all subjects. His knowledge of national and world affairs, science and technological development, law, the arts, and history, among other subjects, was unequaled in my experience. Dates, names, and chronology of events came from him with unbelievable ease and accuracy. Chris was a walking encyclopedia. He had an appreciation of events beyond mere enduring memory. And he brought enlightened interpretation to social issues. Witty and full of life, Chris was an educated man and a truly warm human being. At his burial in his hometown of Nnewi, in eastern Nigeria, I kept asking myself where all that knowledge went. Is there a storehouse of universal knowledge somewhere? Is all of it lost? What can science glean from such endowed lives? I imagine that the same thoughts were the reason for the ongoing fiddling with Albert Einstein's preserved brain by scientists. Will we ever know the real dynamics of intelligence and of the human brain and mind?

Again, I've experienced the passing of many dear friends: our family priest and confidant, the Very Rev. Monsignor Francis Akukwe, a dedicated priest of God who was with us in christenings, in celebrations, and in deaths. Fidelis Okwuosa, dear childhood friend with whom I shared childhood bird-catching expeditions. Professor Edith Elizabeth Lord, a great clinician and my mentor. Richard Onwuka, Dennis Ogbo, Rose Obodo, Patrick Nzeli, Ambrose Chukwujindu, Veronica Akpe. Dr. Nzemeka Oduah, an amiable and generous physician. The Rev I. Eyeye, who married Susan's junior sister. John Anowi, a teacher par excellence. Professor Isidore Eyo, Professor Felicia Ekejiuba, Sylvia Omeogo Ngoddy, the last a lady of unusual beauty, intellect, and charm. Professor Jas Amankulor. Professor Aaron T. Gana, an outstanding scholar and devoted advocate of good governance. Lawrence Onyeagoro, Professor John Ebie, Nnadili Nwakonobi (Oza), Uzii Obiekwe

Alumona, Nwachukwu Patrick Obaze. Good people, people with whom we celebrated life.

One cannot help but be affected even by "distant" deaths. Didn't the poet William Blake, a long time ago, so poignantly muse, "Can I see another's woe and not be in sorrow?"

The distant deaths of John F. Kennedy, Samora Machel, Alastair Cooke (whose erudite and insightful "Letter from America" aired on BBC), Pope John Paul II, Golda Meier, Martin Luther King Jr., John Garang, Jonas Savimbi, Patrice Lumumba, Yassar Arafat, Kwame Nkrumah, Anwar Sadat, and prominent Nigerians such as Alhaji Ahmadu Bello, Major Chukwuma Nzeogwu, Colonel Francis Fajuiyi, Alhaji (Sir) Abubarkar Tafawa Balewa, General J. T. Aguiyi-Ironsi, Aminu Kano, Alhaji Adegoke Adelabu, Dr. Nnamdi Azikiwe, Chief Obafemi Awolowo, and Afro beat musician Fela Anikulakpo-Kuti brought deep personal grief. Even the death of the "unknown" soldier in battle, friend or foe, makes me grieve for a mother, the nine months of total protection, years of love and care, the grooming into adulthood, the hopes and dreams nurtured in a mother's breast, and the irrationality of the wastage of life. When an unknown soldier is felled by a bullet, does anyone care? Some official may mouth routine and convenient condolences, but somewhere, a mother deeply knows and moans, for labor lost.

There was also the very intimate death of my lifelong friend, Dr. Hyacinth Uwaeze Obi-Keguna. Hyacinth and I attended the same secondary school, and upon graduation, we worked in the same department in the Ministry of Agriculture. We studied at the same university for our undergraduate degrees and in the same discipline. We taught in the same department upon the completion of our doctoral programs. Our families and friends considered us inseparable; we had become part of each other's family, each other's life. Family members on both sides often addressed us as "brothers." Then Hyacinth died, and a part of me also died. Truly, John Donne was right when he wrote "Ask not for whom the bell tolls …" Every death diminishes us, some more than others. In contemplating death, I often remember some lines from Professor Edith Lord's poem "The Gravedigger" in her book, *Fragments of Edith Lord*:

I crept to the graveyard late last night
To bury another me
And the gravedigger laughed the while I wept,
And he said, as he dug for me,
"Why do you die by little bits
And bury yourself in parts?
Sensible people die but once,
And I dig a grave for their hearts …"

Do humans really have much of a choice in the matter of death, of dying in little bits, being diminished by each death? The continuity of life in an unceasing flow through reincarnation, the every-where-ness of life, and nature's enduring self-renewal in the seasons with the ebb and resurgence of life from season to season, constitute the African answer to the dilemma of death. Thus, Senegalese poet Birago Diop is able to say:

Those who are dead are never gone:
They are there in the thickening shadow;
The dead are not under the earth:
They are in the tree that rustles,
they are in the wood that groans,
they are in the water that runs,
they are in the water that sleeps,
they are in the hut, they are in the crowd,
they are not dead.

My maternal grandfather, Chief Owelle Uzowulu, a pleasant old man with a quiet smile on his face all the time, had a variety of thought-provoking adages and life sayings. He was fond of saying that "the good thing about death is that it makes living urgent." Young as I was, I couldn't figure this out, but later I recognized that he was speaking about the fruitful use of time, about living life to the fullest. More profoundly, my genial grandpa would say that when your friends and contemporaries are dying off, friends who can call you by your first name with no restraint ("I kpo yi afa ikekele eze," in Igbo), that is, in total familiarity, you should begin to reflect more seriously on eternity and your upcoming role as an ancestor, seek to mend broken fences, and plan a few goodbyes.

Chapter 9

Of Nature and Nature Things

In childhood, the marvels of nature fascinated me. They still do. Flowers, trees, animals, insects, running brooks, everything alive, all did and still carry an enduring hold on me. As a young child, I delighted in keeping all manner of pets, including lizards, earthworms, crickets, and even small rats. But birds have held my interest the longest, especially canaries. Some of my friends liked them too. We kept canaries for their song, and in Kano, we also kept them for competitions. You could earn some money if your bird beat another bird in a singing competition. There is a long stretch of canary sound (chrrriiiiiiiiiiiii), which follows several twittering sounds. That is counted as one point, and the bird with the highest number of such stretches in a specified time frame, is considered the winner. Mostly, I kept my canaries for the private enjoyment of their song and to watch them prancing around in their cage, appearing quite joyful. We often gave them fresh red pepper, which they liked, and it seemed to make them sing better. Now past seventy, I still have the excitement of keeping birds. I have not outgrown the urge.

At the University of Nigeria in Nsukka, I kept the only private aviary in town. It was a beautiful one, with canaries, varieties of wild pigeons, doves, and others. A set of canaries built nests and laid eggs in the aviary, but for some reason, the eggs did not hatch. It must be that the birds were missing some necessary nutrients that they were not getting in the feed we provided. Or perhaps, the human traffic back and forth disturbed their routine of sitting on their eggs. Many bird lovers from Enugu and elsewhere would come to see the aviary. One particular individual, a professor of medicine, D. C. Nwafo, himself an avid lover of birds, would come to take a look each time he came to Nsukka from Enugu, and he continues to ask me about my aviary, years after I left the town.

I had an interesting experience with a species of wild pigeons. I bought a set of brown pigeons (male and female) from the town of Jos in northern Nigeria while I was there for a conference and put them in my aviary. One day, another set of pigeons that was nesting in a tree behind our home, was disturbed by a rainstorm, and their nest fell to the ground with the two young ones still inside. It was not possible to put the nest in the tree again because of the foliage, and we were not sure the parents would tend to them after we had handled them. Some birds reject their young ones if they are touched by others. I kept the two little birds in their nest inside my aviary and fed them a mixture of milk and chicken feed.

One evening, while my daughter Lillian was plaiting a friend's hair by the side of the aviary, she called out to say that the bigger birds were near the little birds' nest, and perhaps they might hurt them. I and a group of people in the house ran out and what we saw was absolutely thrilling. The big birds were actually feeding the little ones, and so I did not have to feed them myself. This was my first experience of within-species feeding of young birds by other birds that were not their own natural parents. Remember that the older birds had been brought down to Nsukka from Jos in the north, a distance of more than six hundred kilometers. It was a fascinating experience, and some neighbors made pilgrimages to see this miracle of two adult birds feeding young ones that were not their own.

I had another interesting experience with cross-species parenting, when our aged dog, Lassy, breastfed our young cat, named Lira, and in all purposes became its mother. We'd brought this young cat from the village, some forty kilometers away. One could see droplets of milk after each feeding. It was surprising because Lassy was old and had her last litter of puppies over four years before. Lassy shared food and played games with the cat, dispelling for me the old adage of cat and dog incompatibility. In addition, with this relationship, Lassy became more vibrant, gained weight and regained her lost hair. I published these exciting observations of Lassy and Lira in a scientific psychology journal with pictures that showed the play, feeding and grooming activity between the two animals.

Back to birds; I have always had a way with birds. When we moved from Nekede back to Enugu, I took my weaverbird with me. A pair of two-day-old almost featherless weaverbirds had been brought to me by someone who knew that I was a lover of birds. (In the neighborhood, they nicknamed me "Nna Nnunu"---father of birds). I raised the little birds all by myself on some concoction that I prepared. One died, but the other survived and became homebound. We named her Genie. When we moved to Enugu, we stayed in an upstairs flat, and I set up a small nesting area for it. She would fly out and come back for her meals when I was back from work. She perched on my head or shoulder and ate off my hands or off the children's plates as the children were eating.

Susan and children did not move immediately with me to Enugu as she was ending her own responsibilities as headmistress of the Holy Rosary School in Owerri. She also had just had our boy, Onyechi Leonard. I was therefore initially all alone. Before Susan and the children joined me, my new neighbors in Enugu did not know what to make of a young man whose only companion was a weaverbird. One of them said I was an *Ofuogoli* (irresponsible person). Once, Genie flew out, and some young boys caught her and shouted that they had caught a bird. But someone told them to let the bird go, that she belonged to me. They let her go, and she flew right back home. I asked the boys to come and be friends with Genie and feed her, and they enjoyed themselves doing this. Genie had become part of our lives and the lives of neighborhood children. She lived to a ripe old age. We gave her a family burial as we usually do with our pets. And there were tears.

In recent years, though, I have become, strangely, rather queasy about keeping birds. This became even more problematic after I negligently let my pet canary die because I did not fill its water bin. I was upset for some time. But even before then I had begun to reflect on the freedom of birds; the catchy title of Maya Angelou's beautiful book on the black American experience, *I Know Why the Caged Bird Sings*, often comes to mind. I began to worry about the freedom I was denying the birds. Cats and dogs I have no difficulty with because they live free.

Sometimes, I have let my birds go after a while, just to let them live free. One kite kept coming back for some years. It would perch on the fence demanding food and would respond to my imitation of its call. It finally flew away and, I hope, found its niche in the bird world. My prayer was that it would not get killed before it had become fully acclimatized to the wild. During my childhood, when any of my canaries escaped and flew away, I really enjoyed the experience of seeing them go. Rather than feel sad, I often felt tremendous joy and exhilaration, as if I had flown away with them into space and I would describe the event joyfully to my friends! One canary escaped but continued to return to sleep in its cage, which I kept open.

Well, now I have found a way of having an aviary as part of my home environment. I just leave some water bins around and keep a few feeding troughs in apprpriate places, and varieties of birds will flock to the compound. All you need is a strategic watching position, and you get the pleasure of watching a variety of birds. Some small river birds also visit Susan's fishpond, occasionally. If you have some fruit trees in the compound, then your "aviary" will be real fun. And sometimes the birds don't fly away in a hurry but walk away as you open the door to go out or build nests in the small flower plants by your exit door and don't fly off even when you open the door noisily. That means that they have accepted your presence and are in harmony with you. In fact, even the neighborhood lizards soon learn not to scamper away when you appear and take their time to go away or even ignore your presence. One downside was when a fish-eater bird, an *Nkenu* built its nest in a hole in our fishpond and ate up most of the little fish! It was doing its own fishing in our pond!

I love bird songs. Don't we all? It is a most joyful experience to wake up to the songs of the *Okili-mgbama* or, the cooing of the *kpanakuku* (the brown pigeon), the songs of the *Nduli* (the wild dove), the waking chirping of the tiny nectar-sucking *nza* (mockingbird). Early morning travelers hooting their horns and noisy motorcycles are rude interruptions that distort nature's harmonic awakening. The songs that start around six o'clock in the morning are different from the evening calls. The early morning song of the *Okili-mgbama* sounds very much like "time to wake, time to wake" with an elongated one sounding like "time to wake, time to wake, to wake." Or, perhaps, it is really "time to work." There is a sense of the same meaning in Igbo language, with the songs sounding like "te-ta, te ta," meaning "wake up, wake up." After a number of "calls to wake" by the leading bird, there is a fast chatter from several birds as if in chorus. Then a brief silence, before the leader bird renders some more calls to wake, followed by chorus chatters. No other birds usually interrupt their singing routine. Once their work is done, other bird species then seem to feel free to begin their own morning songs. To go to bed with the songs of the night birds mingled with the various insect sounds ringing in the head, is to feel the very essence of nature's gifts. The *Obu's* early night bass rendering is soothing. Even the hooting of the *Okwikwi* (the night owl) in the late hours of the night or the approaching twilight, is a reminder of the continuity of life, of the morning to come. The cockcrow, that universal sound summoning the new dawn, is blissful to wake up to. These and the serenity of the village engender a wonderful feeling of peacefulness that I rarely find elsewhere.

Along the riverbanks in my hometown Atani, along the tributaries of the Niger, one is delighted with the sight of unbelievable colors of the river birds. There is the plumage of the *Ebebe* (the wild ducks); the dramatic dance and positioning of the fish eater birds, the *Okwoli*, the *Odumisi*, and especially the *Nkenu* while stalking their prey in the waters below. Then there is the leggy walk of the flamingos, all displaying the elegance of the creations of the Supreme Artist and all of them sources of unbelievable ecstasy. Sometimes, it seems like sacrilege to shoot, kill, and pluck the feathers off these astounding creatures to get to their flesh. Well, I have always been squeamish about animal life. I am not able to eat any animal I raise and, right now, I am unable to eat fish from Susan's small fishpond. This has been with me for a long time. I recall that when we were at Nekede farm, I would raise quite a lot of poultry, but I usually gave them away and bought the ones we ate from the market. It sounds silly because the ones we ate had the same bird life! Yet, knowing that it's silly doesn't stop me even now from being queasy. Having fed the ones in my care, and they would run or fly toward me when I called or whistled, it always feels cruel to kill them and, worse still, to eat them. Once, I tried and threw up.

Sometimes, I have to watch myself. I have become so protective of birds that I have noticed myself preventing the grandchildren from taking away young birds from their nests, a popular childhood activity. They attempt to raise them as I did in my time. I have to ask myself to let them have their own experiences in the hope that, in time, they also may become enamored of nature and bestow on nature their own special appreciation of life.

Years ago, I wrote a little piece in appreciation of nature titled, "When It's over."

When it's over
In the long, long forever
Not you, not you
Man, not just you

There's the rising sun
The setting sun
Moonshine at night
Early morn twilight
Shimmering river flow
Groves and shrubbery a-glow

A rosebud gently unfolds
Sharing its aroma and allure
A mother hen a hatchling chick beholds
Those first steps unsure
A tiny seed
Sprouts a giant tree
All earth's wonders sublimely feed
Our senses free

Oh, to watch butterflies flutter
And hear insects twitter

Azubike Uzoka

Little fish gracefully swim
Chirping birds sing
In concordant ring
With earth's sonorous hymn

A rainbow streaks across the sky
Sight so noble and sweet to see
A gentle wind creates a tender sigh
I wonder if it's all for me
All nature's gifts in bounteous splendor
I claim them all in this life-long tour.

So when it's all over
In that long, long forever
Not you, not you
Man, not just you
For in that forever future
Is the absence of all nature.

Chapter 10

Frights in Life

Everyone, at sometime, has experienced fear and other deep and frightening emotions. As I grew up, I was, unlike other children of my age, not afraid of the dark. Rather, I found and still find darkness comforting. It shuts out the world and lets you be all by yourself. There are no shadows, no unwanted visual reminders of the world; just you, yourself, and the invited guests in your mind. You shut mind's gates when un-invited, un-welcome guests knock. Then, before slumber, there is the anticipated world of dreams. Darkness is tranquil and soothing unless one has corpses or rattling skeletons in mind's crevices and catacombs.

However, I have had my share of frightening situations. Once, while standing by my car, a dog lunged at me. We had heard that two wild dogs were about. When that one lunged at me, I felt real fear. But I stood my ground; when it came close, I kicked it up in the air, and it fell down. It got up and lunged at me the second time. This time, I kicked it so hard it fell on top of the car nearby and ran away. Two days later, it was found dead. The veterinary personnel determined that it had rabies. Immediately after the event I found myself shaking, even though I did not display the experience of being frightened during the attack.

While on a diplomatic trip to Guyana, our plane, a British Viscount model, I believe, created quite a stir when it approached the capital, Georgetown. First, it had some unstated problem, and we had to stay in the air for some time. Then, another problem was identified. Based on the pilot's calculations, the tires would not descend in readiness for landing. The pilot had tested the relevant controls without success. We were in the air for another length of time. There was panic in the plane. The crew could not control the panic, probably because they were also visibly agitated and distraught. Their training for equanimity in such circumstances seemed to have left them. Later I was to wonder why they let the passengers know what the problems were that caused such agitation all over the plane since, ordinarily, the crew usually spared passengers such detail. Along on the diplomatic mission were Dr. Okechukwu Ikejiani and Professor Kalu Ezera. Professor Ezera and I were in considerable distress, but Dr. Ikejiani was calm and apparently indifferent to the happenings. He called for drinks, and the air hostess could not understand such a request given the circumstances, although she served the drinks. I joined Dr. Ikejiani in taking the gin and tonic.

I felt frightened but detached from the furor, as if it didn't matter if the plane crashed. My initial sense of fright turned into something of a stoic acceptance and quiet resolve. Perhaps it was a denial of sorts. Or perhaps the gin/tonic brew had begun to take effect. Maybe they should serve alcoholic drinks in such situations. A belly landing on some sand stretch—I don't recall whether it was on a coast line—was announced. Eventually, just before the pilot dumped the fuel in preparation for the emergency landing, he found that the tires could be released, and we were able to land normally. When we settled into our hotel, the whole experience left me numb and I realized that I was experiencing delayed reaction to fright.

Once, in friendship, and fully aware of the possible consequences, I put myself in a frightening situation in Miami. I was frightened even before I took on the activity. I had become friends with one of the doctors in the university medical center on campus. His name was Dr. McBrayer. He was a pediatrician who got into general practice and often joked about why he switched. He said pediatrics was quite a cumbersome specialty. First, the doctor had to keep his door open all day and night; then he would be woken up by frightened parents, usually mothers, in the middle of the night, carrying their sick babies. On top of this, the doctor had patients who could not themselves say what was wrong with them!

Good natured and humorous, Dr. McBrayer was the one who first pointed out the cause of my regular ailments; he identified them as allergies. Eventually I discovered I was allergic to onions and crayfish. Warm and soft-spoken, Dr. McBrayer had lost his first wife several years earlier, remarried at an advanced age, and had two delightful little girls who were in primary school. He doted on them. They were the joy of his life. He always looked forward to parent-teacher meetings and would not miss the children's school activities for any reason. Then my friend had an accident and broke one or two rib bones. After several months of treatment, the wound failed to heal, and follow-up evaluation revealed that he had lung cancer that had spread through the rib cage without his knowledge. That was his major puzzle. "How could I have had no signs at all?" he kept asking. He was a heavy smoker, and it wasn't the cancer that surprised him, only its silent nature. After a few months, he became homebound. He was stoic about it all, but he was in so much pain. Sometime later, he could not even lie in bed without experiencing excruciating pain. He had to spend his time in a chair that was set up to accommodate his condition and bring him some relief.

Now, this is the story of my adventure with fright. Dr. McBrayer abhorred the medications that kept him sedated. All he wanted was to be able to see, hold, and play with his beloved little girls. You should see his joy as he held them, even as he battled the excruciating pain. On one of my frequent visits, he said, "Felix, I need help. I need your help. I don't want to be sedated anymore and the only option I have is to get some marijuana, which, I believe, will help me with the pain without sedation. Please obtain some for me."

I reacted strongly to his request, saying, "Me, obtain marijuana? Listen, dear, I have no idea whatsoever how to set about getting marijuana. You already know that." We both laughed and he said that we were two old-fashioned people who had very little contact with the youth culture. We exchanged ideas about how to get about obtaining the stuff. Nothing clicked. He was as "unconnected" as I was! His agony touched me to the core. He was such a great guy. He did not need to persuade me to assist him. The warmth of our friendship was enough persuasion. I was in agony over his condition.

Fortuitously, when I went to the office about two days later, I overheard a conversation about marijuana. Two of my colleagues, who I had not known were users, were discussing the cost of the stuff! I quickly took one of them aside and explained my friend's plight. She knew I did not use the stuff and laughed about how naïve I was. "Isn't the whole town awash with the stuff?" she exclaimed. She volunteered to obtain some for me. The next day, she brought two small polythene bags containing marijuana, at no expense to me. I got her to drop the stuff in the trunk of my car. I was too scared to even touch it. My disposition might seem unusually reactive, but remember I was a foreign student, aware of the existing penalties for possessing marijuana. I sat in my office, pondering how to get the stuff to my friend. I was fortunate that day because I had no clients scheduled; I would have been quite inefficient if I had. Getting from the office to Dr. McBrayer's home in Coral Gables was a real nightmare. What would happen to me and my family if I got caught with the stuff? Who would believe my story? I imagined myself in a police cell and a trial followed by imprisonment and deportation. I don't believe I did any significant work for the rest of that day. At the end of the workday, I drove with trepidation toward my friend's home, nerves on edge. Along the way, a police siren sounded, and I began to pull over, thinking he was ordering me to stop, but the police van sped on its way. With sweat all over me, I eventually reached my destination and with great relief, I asked my friend's wife to come and pick up the stuff from the car. I still didn't want to touch it. That was some nerve-racking day for me. My recompense was the great relief that my friend appeared to experience from using the stuff, and the joy I had watching him play with his dear little girls before he passed on.

I always prided myself on having some sense of calm, some measure of control in troubled situations, even before my university education in psychology. That was why I had difficulty understanding why I went berserk and uncontrollable the day I nearly killed my grandson with a car that had rolled out of control. I started the car and revved to go backward but did not know that my grandson was playing behind. When I saw the danger and tried to stop the car, it failed to stop; the brakes failed or perhaps I momentarily lost my driving sense, and the car rolled dangerously toward the youngster. Providence, I believe, prevented the catastrophe, because in my fear and fright I lost total composure and was shaking. It had to be providence because someone observed the potential tragedy and shouted at the boy, who instinctively jumped aside so that the approaching car merely grazed his arm. Two days afterward, I was still unable to recover from my fright, and even now when I remember the event, I shudder. And I acquired a neurotic tendency to make an unduly long inspection of the environment and to keep looking back when reversing a car, even in an empty, open field!

Chapter 11

Acting and Real Life

"All the world is a stage and all the men and women merely players ..."
William Shakespeare

Reality. Reality. What is real? Could the old sage be right about life being a mere play or script? Frankly, I often wonder about what is real and what is not.

I have always loved the theater. I grew up with the cinema, the old-time cinema, with showings from 8 p.m. to 12 a.m. or 1 a.m. Later, I went into acting under the aegis of the British Council in Enugu. The council sponsored the Eastern Nigeria Theatre Group, later named the Ogui Players. The British Council was an excellent motivator for many of the young men and women in Enugu, in terms of educational pursuits. I read so many of the novels and theme books in its extensive library. For theater, some British nationals served as our coaches, directors, and producers before Nigerians took over. John Ekwere was our director/producer at the time we performed John Pepper Clark's *Song of a Goat.* In that play, I was Tonye, and Alice, a stunningly beautiful and talented young lady, played Ebiere, the wife of Tonye's elder brother.

While we were acting in *Song of a Goat,* Alice and I fell in love with each other or perhaps became infatuated with each other. We became close beyond the demands of the scenes we acted, holding hands, spending time alone away from the troupe, sharing confidences, looking into each other's eyes, and feeling good about our togetherness. A dalliance seemed inevitable. I think there is only a thin line between infatuation and love. I am not sure

77

that the difference between these two states of mind is always clear. Perhaps it is that love endures beyond the physical, while infatuation ends or quickly diminishes with sexual gratification and familiarity.

In *Song of a Goat*, Tonye seduced his elder brother's wife, Ebiere. Actually, as the script was written, it was Ebiere who seduced Tonye. With the acting, Alice and I became so fond of each other that we had to sit down and frankly discuss the boundaries of the play and our personal lives. Alice was beautiful, well beyond the physical, supremely graceful in mind and body. It was difficult to be around her without feeling the rapture of ennobled womanhood. She was intelligent and could debate anyone on practically any subject. She was well read. She also thought well of me, perhaps because I served as the prompt for the group and also functioned as her prompt, now and again. Alice was married, with children. I too was married with children. Most of the guys in the troupe were after her, and I was the object of considerable jealousy because they thought Alice and I were on. We were the objects of jibes and jokes.

Why is it that when acting, emotions often become real and felt and not just imaginary or fictional? Is it due to inexperience? When one is immersed in a part or role, the emotions truly come alive and one actually is able to shed tears in such contrived situations. One day, after an emotionally charged scene in a play, one of the actresses could not stop her tears and someone went up to her and said, "Look, girl, it's only a play, ordinary make-believe." Well, for me and for a good number of my fellow actors, it often did not feel like make-believe.

Indeed, life on stage takes on a reality of its own and calls up the appropriate emotions for each occasion. I doubt that anyone can act truly well without the appropriate emotions arising in him or her and finding expression. I imagine that the beauty and thrill of giving expression to life's universal and unique encounters, remains the fun and appeal of theater, a process that seeks to creatively and dramatically mirror life's primordial realities. Anyway, in later years, observing the checkered family lives of many Hollywood actors and actresses, I was happy I did not stay with the theater. In any case, except for the Ogunde theater troupe, theater in Nigeria was then in its infancy, and most participants saw the activity merely as a pastime. The booming Nigerian film industry, Nollywood, has come too late for me, but I do get the itch even now.

Chapter 12

Early University Education

I had dreams of attending a university, but given my circumstances, it was a far-fetched dream. I had passed the advanced level papers in the General Certificate of Education of the University of London in 1956/57 and therefore was qualified for direct entry into a university. But finances were the problem. Susan and I were paying a portion of the school fees for our siblings. One of my sisters, Uzoamaka Stella, was living with us. Many times, we were broke, penniless. Sometimes, we did not have even six pence to buy corn meal (*Akamu*) for our young daughter Adaeze-Susan, and we had to borrow. In fact, I believe that Adaeze's development was affected by the poor feeding we gave her in her early days. So, going to the university was a pipe dream.

I tried various employment options, at different times considering joining the Nigerian Police Force or the Nigerian Prisons Service as an assistant superintendent-in-training, both senior staff positions. Susan said no to these suggestions. She said she did not bargain on marrying a uniformed person! I, too, do not much like uniforms and have aversion to standing out and being noticed. This was to affect my involvement in the knighthood in the church. When I was invited to join both the Knights of St. Mulumba and the Knights of St. John International, the idea of wearing a uniform was (besides my sense of personal and spiritual inadequacy) the major constraint, although I eventually was persuaded to join the Knights of St. Mulumba by very determined friends. One of them said to me, "The knighthood is not for saints; it is for ordinary people who strive harder for moral and spiritual elevation"

My friend Hyacinth and I remained consumed with the dream of university education. It did not help that some young men we worked with, those who had the means, would go off to the University of Ibadan or overseas for three years or so, come back with their degrees, and become our bosses. At that time, the academic school calendar in the universities (there were only two of them in Nigeria then) was strictly adhered to, and graduation time was fixed and regular. Much more painful, the returning graduates would hold discussions in an esoteric language, mentioning Aristotle, Plato, Confucius, and other such names, and we would be left in the cold. They really showed off. One day, standing in front of Hyacinth's residence, we decided to apply for admission to the University of Nigeria, which had advertised for candidates. We agreed we should just apply and get admitted, so we could prove that we could do it. It had become a matter of pride. We had no hope of sponsorship. We applied, nonetheless.

Then I broached the subject with my Uncle Luke. He said it was a good idea but worried about how we would manage paying my fees as well as those of my siblings and the other members of the family. In fact, another uncle's son, Ifeanyi, was living with me in Enugu. I told my uncle that I had applied for a federal scholarship and had attended an interview for the scholarship. We agreed that should my application be successful, Susan would contribute as much as possible to the family expenses and we also discussed the possibility of a loan arranged by the family. When the admission lists were released, Hyacinth and I were offered admission. My uncle saw the advertisement in the newspapers and called me to Onitsha. He was initially upset with the course I had chosen, psychology. He had urged me to read law and expected me to be the first Attorney in the family. But psychology appealed to me. He asked me why, and I told him I had read a book on psychology in his small library and became enthused with the subject. In the end, he said, "If you obtain a scholarship, I will manage with your wife to continue to maintain our relatives in school and we will also explore the possibility of a loan."

We agreed to do that. In the meantime, I tried to cash in on the goodwill I thought I had by approaching a well-known businessman/transporter I had helped in my position as head of stores. I'd even assisted him when some functionaries of the party in power, the National Council of Nigeria and the Cameroon, gave an order that he should not be given supply contracts anymore because he was allegedly fighting the party. He begged me to give the supply contracts to his wife instead. I did. I even allowed him other privileges, such as allowing him to reuse the disposable raffia bags that had become property of the department for packaging grain. I was pleased with his execution of supply contracts compared to others, who delayed their contracts and caused us considerable difficulty in the timely preparation and distribution of animal feeds. When he was supplying material to my stores, he often sought to give me gratification but I rejected such offers. I was partial to him because of the efficiency he exhibited in his work with us; for me, that was enough gratification.

I assured Hyacinth that we would be able to obtain loans from him. When we got to his house, he barely welcomed us. After I presented the reason for our presence, he blurted out, "I have no money to lend you." We had asked for a loan of £60 sterling apiece, which we planned to repay with interest. I left his house in utter shame. I had assured Hyacinth that this man—who previously had offered me £1,000 sterling, a plot of land, and a finished building, offers that I rejected—would be delighted to give me a loan of £60 and another £60 to him. We were disappointed and left in shame. Later, I learned from his associate that he said that he had stopped supplying grains and in any case, since I was about to leave the service, I was of no use to him anymore!

Anyway, we enrolled in the university in September. I registered with the possibility that if I did not obtain a scholarship, I would probably withdraw. I registered with the last money Susan and I had. Hyacinth had success with his brother-in-law, Godwin Onyegbula, who was then a senior civil servant and later became a permanent secretary, an ambassador in the Nigerian Foreign Service, and head of the Biafran Foreign Ministry during the Nigeria-Biafra conflict. Onyegbula offered to sponsor Hyacinth with what Hyacinth believed was a loan. However, when Hyacinth graduated and went to discuss the repayment, Onyegbula dismissed him, saying that the money was a gift. Hyacinth said that Onyegbula made light of the matter, asking whether he looked like a moneylender. Such unbelievable generosity, such largeness of the heart.

With uncertainties over school fees, and having been out of school for about nine years, I had initial difficulties with schoolwork. I found some of the younger students intimidating. When questions were asked, some of the young ones in class would rattle off the correct answers before I even comprehended what had been asked. Two of the brightest were Regina Nnacheta, a pretty and vivacious young girl (now Dr. Eya) and Henry Amatu. When I went to Enugu for the weekend, I told Susan about my plight. I told her that going to school was an experiment and that I would opt out if it became too bad. I ended by saying, "I am going to run away to the Cameroon to seek employment. How can I face all those people at work with the stigma of failure?"

Susan encouraged me to stick to it. She said, "You know more than you give yourself credit for." I was consoled, and went back to school with a bit more courage. As it turned out, when the results of the first semester examinations were published, I had the best result. As a consequence, I was offered the university scholarship. One day, while celebrating the scholarship offer, I saw my brother, Okwudili, who had entered the university a year before me, running toward me from the Margaret Ekpo Refectory in great excitement. "Brother, brother," he shouted, "You have won the federal scholarship; your name is in the newspaper, the *Daily Times.*"

He shoved the newspaper at me. I stood transfixed. I could not believe my good fortune. I was not used to winning or getting anything for which I did not truly labor. I never win at sweepstakes or lotteries. In the event, I gave up the university scholarship for the more enhanced federal grant. With it, if I were frugal, I still would be able to contribute to the extended family expenses. That was the beginning of a wonderful undergraduate experience.

My financial problems for school had come to an end. And, by again obtaining the best results in the final examinations for the year, I earned an overseas trip. I joined students from other departments on the annual summer trip to Michigan State University in East Lansing. Michigan State University was the mentoring university to which the University of Nigeria was affiliated. The trip was a reward for excellent academic performance, granted every year to deserving students. That was my first trip overseas, and it was truly a rewarding experience. I took some summer courses and did pretty well.

One of the experiences that stuck in my mind happened during a class for a course in urban sociology at Michigan State University. The professor was an elderly but sprightly man, perhaps in his late sixties or early seventies. One day, he was explaining a concept and, to my mind, was quite lucid in what he was saying. However, a tiny young Caucasian girl sitting up front, wearing cut-off jeans, so short you could see her pubic hair, and with her legs propped up on the front desk, interrupted the professor and said, "You are not making sense."

I thought I'd heard wrong, but she repeated herself a second time. I felt like disappearing from the room. I was in fright for the girl. Back home, you did not say things like that to your teacher. You couched your questions or comments in respectful language. But the old, gray-haired professor did not seem troubled by the girl's comment or by the tenor of its presentation. He took his time to again explain the concept he was presenting in great detail and, at the end of a long explanation, the young lady said; "Now you are talking."

I went back to my hostel that evening, pondering the young lady's audacity and the fact that her demeanor raised no eyebrows among the entire class and no displeasure from the professor. It was my first taste of American freedom. But forgive me. Even as I write, I am convinced that in any other culture outside the United States, the young girl's manner would be considered impolite. Perhaps, this was some product of the simmering youth revolt and evolving youth culture of the 1960s. Or, was I unfamiliar with the language that was acceptable in the culture? Something else that caught my attention was the fact that at two o'clock in the morning, the sun would be up. It was complete daylight. I'd had no experience of summer solstice before then, and I would wake up, start walking around and find nobody. Everybody was asleep.

We had fun trips to various areas around Michigan, including Saginaw, several large farms, and the Kellogg factory where cornflakes are made. A cousin of mine, Patrick Obi Ngoddy (now a distinguished professor of agricultural engineering) was then studying at Michigan State University. He and his friends made us feel at home and provided us meals similar to our traditional meals. Some of us could not handle the hamburgers and other American food for some time. For those of us used to a heavy carbohydrate intake, the scanty rice or potatoes in the meals were not filling or satisfying at all. Overall, however, the Michigan experience was a wonderful one.

E. W. Findlay, one of my bosses from my days in the Ministry of Agriculture, contacted me from his home in Canada. We had nostalgic recollections of our days in the ministry. He had fond memories of his work in Nigeria, and I could see he wished he had stayed on much longer to help bolster agriculture. He asked about the farm settlements that were the backbone of Premier Michael Okpara's agricultural reforms in the eastern region and felt sad that they had been abandoned. He worried that the country would pay a price in food security if we slid backward in agricultural development. Subsequent events have proven him right.

By the time we returned to Nigeria, school had become comfortable, and I was able to take on extracurricular engagements. I was elected president of the Psychology Students Association and chairman for the Eyo Ita Hall of Residence at the University of Nigeria. One of the privileges was that I could stay in one room all by myself, although most chairmen had one roommate. I had wonderful guys at different times as roommates. One was Stephen Udoh, enrolled for statistics, a decent gentleman. Another was Alphonsus Ndupu. Like me, he was married. He was a decent, considerate person, and he was a bookworm. He did not like my study habits. Because of the good fortune of an excellent memory, I did not have to labor at various subjects, unless they were mathematics or statistics. During examinations, he would wake me up for the umpteenth time, saying in Oguta Igbo, "I guwo di akukwo?" (Won't you study?) I would plead with him to wake me up in another hour or so. He got fed up with me and left me to my fate.

We had excellent teachers. There was John Anowi, a developmental psychologist whose teaching was so down to earth, so practical; he was a teacher par excellence. I believe I coped rather well in my postgraduate studies in the United States because of his lucid teaching. And then there were two

American professors. Carl Frost taught industrial/organizational psychology and acted in the capacity of deputy vice chancellor of the university from time to time. Edith Elizabeth Lord was a consummate clinical psychologist who inspired me greatly. Her influence resulted in my choosing the clinical field of specialization. There was also Dr. Kalu Aja, with whom I had so many academic disputations (pleasant ones). Quite a few times, I told him I found something in the journals in the library that contradicted his position. He really challenged me, intellectually. He enjoyed my enthusiastic arguments, even though I was not always right. Dr. Aja later joined the Nigerian Air Force as a personnel officer. We also had an inspiring English teacher in the General Studies program named Dr. Okoreafia, who taught the Use of English course. Before him, my presentations were copious and often wide ranging. But he gave a recipe for writing that I found most useful. He said, "When you are writing anything—theses, essays, even a letter—follow these guidelines, One, say very briefly what you want to say. Two, say it as precisely as possible. Three, say that you have said it."

"Waste no words" was his catch phrase. Don't waste any words, don't ramble, and do not use any irrelevant words or ideas. I always have this injunction at the back of my mind when making any presentation, although sometimes I end up leaving out significant details. I try to remain guided by the general principle of being as precise as possible in every presentation, although I am not sure I succeed often enough.

Nsukka was truly a university town. There was little else around but the university. Nestled between beautiful green hills that Professor Emmanuel Obiechina called "breasts" in his poetry, there was a calm serene air around the town. In fact, some people have argued that the comfort of the town often "imprisoned" its dwellers and made them unwilling to seek to live or work elsewhere, even when there were better paying jobs elsewhere. The weather was temperate, and some nights were rather cold. It was also a town that allowed for easy sanitation because of its hilly and rocky terrain. The Honorable Dr. Nnamdi Azikiwe, the founder of the university, knew what he was doing in choosing the location. In fact, he had his primary country home there, and his presence in the town provided additional incentive for seeking excellence. The campus was well laid out, and students had good meals and the university provided staff to maintain the students' hostels.

We had problems with poisonous snakes, however. The whole environment seemed infested with them. These were vipers known as *echi ete ka* in Igbo and *gwobe de nisa* in Hausa (both names mean "tomorrow is too far"). This was because the victims often died within hours of snakebite. The doctors had great difficulty with snakebites, especially those that were not on the legs or arms but on the torso because they could not apply tourniquets, if necessary, or immerse the body part in ice, as was done sometimes. Such bites occurred when students laid down on the grassy lawn at night for play or for romantic purposes. But some students were bitten in the toilet and bathroom areas.

Dr. Ohaeri, the clinic doctor, discovered how the native doctors successfully treated the snake bites using traditional methods. He eventually published his findings in a manuscript. According to Dr. Ohaeri, the process was one of "post-bite" inoculation or immunization. The story was that the native doctors would catch the female snakes that were pregnant and by taunting make them really angry, thus ensuring that the heads would be full of venom. Then the heads would be cut off instantly and placed to dry in the sun or on rafts high above the cooking fireplace. Subsequently, the native doctors would grind the dried snakeheads and apply them, along with some special leaves, on bite sites. The area around the bite sites would be mildly slashed open in several places with razor blades prior to this application. This "inoculation," applied after snakebites, was known to be more effective than the Western treatments that were available at the time. Many more of the snakebite victims survived under the care of the native doctors than with the university medical center, leading Dr. Ohaeri to seek to determine the reason for their success.

The atmosphere in my department and in the university generally was disciplined and focused on academics. Those were the days when real academic culture existed in the universities. The students fraternized with each other and worked together. We were serious at scholarship. At the end of it all, I was happy to obtain a first-class honors degree (summa cum laude). I also won several awards including "best student" in my department and "best student" in the Faculty of Social Sciences. Uncle Luke was so excited that he held a party to entertain all his staff at Modebe Memorial School. Clearly he had forgiven me for not reading law. I wish he were here today to see the family filled with lawyers, men and women, including his own son, Dubem. We had emergency graduation as the Nigerian Civil War was looming. The graduation was a hasty, hurried proceeding, held without the usual pomp and pageantry. Indeed, it was more or less an "under a tree" affair. But we were all happy to have become university graduates, ceremony or no ceremony. I went back to my job in the Ministry of Agriculture with a degree in psychology. I was promoted to a senior administrative cadre, and then the civil war broke out.

Chapter 13

A Bit More on Education: The Color of Prejudice

Primary school education was a breeze for me and included one double promotion. I loved school, I loved sports, and I loved my teachers. Oh, and I remember also being in love with one of my female teachers, madly in love. I begged to carry her bag, to see her off, to answer her questions, to hold her hands. Puppy love, indeed, and it felt good. Who said little ones can't fall in love? Mrs. Nwachie thought I was brilliant, because according to her, I wrote good business letters. I had no illusions about my capabilities. I thought I was quite ordinary in scholarship, yet there was something I couldn't deny, that is, that I had a good retentive memory and did quite well in school.

I had some significant experiences in secondary school that I can recall vividly. I was in my fourth year in secondary school at the Metropolitan College, Onitsha. (My mother, in jest, called the school "Mentholatum College," mimicking the name of a brand of balm.) I had a very good English and literature teacher. Later he went overseas and when he returned, he joined the Eastern Nigeria civil service and rose to the rank of accountant-general. His name was John Ibeziako. In school, we usually were given assignments to write essays (then called composition) at home and submit them in class. But each time I wrote an essay, Mr. Ibeziako would write "copied" on top of the essay and refuse to grade it. Worse still, he would stand me up in class as an example of people who copied essays from other sources. That was painful; and I felt great shame, especially because I knew I did not copy from any source.

Unfortunately for me, Uncle Luke, a teacher himself, chided me for copying. "You are good enough with your English. Why do you copy?" he would say. He, of course, believed his fellow teacher. I got so infuriated that I summoned the courage and reported the matter to the principal, P. O. Chude, whom we called without affection, "Iki." His English name was Patrick, and in jest his colleagues used the last three letters of his name as a nickname, calling him "Ick-ick." Gradually it metamorphosed from "Ick-ick" to "Iki." But the students did not know of its origin and did not use it with any kind of affection. For them, the nickname was a derogatory appellation because of the disciplinary strictures he placed on us. I learned of the real meaning of the nickname much later, after graduation from the school. In adult life, many of us began to appreciate his wholesome effect on us, and in his old age we made pilgrimages to his home to thank and honor him for the discipline he taught us.

Anyway, we were then all terrified of Iki. Anyone who attended Metropolitan College from its inception to the early 1970s, has a story or two to tell about Iki. His whippings were both dramatic and fierce. He was a disciplinarian from the old school. But my suffering at being called an essay copier was strong enough to overcome any trepidation. So I went into the principal's office, with a mixture of anger and fright. He said, "Young man, what is your problem? "

I blurted out, near to tears, "I write my compositions, I do not copy, but the teacher says I copy and I am punished at home because of that."

He, of course, knew everybody's name. So, he said to me, "Felix, go. I will find out about it." Whatever he found out resulted in an action that solved the problem for me. Instead of asking the students to prepare essays at home, the teacher was apparently now required to come on Saturdays and administer essay examinations to us. We wrote the essay in class and both the teacher and principal judged my essay as the best. The teacher was unhappy that he had been called to work on Saturdays, but his subsequent behavior gave me one of my first experiences of humility, goodwill, and graciousness. Mr. Ibeziako came to class and apologized for punishing me in the past. He did not stop there. He gave me a Parker pen as a gift. He requested for my earlier essays which he graded and awarded me As, except one which he graded B, because of a punctuation error; a comma was wrongly placed. He began to take special interest in me, and when I finished school and he was in government, he gave me his books, which I used to read for my advanced level papers for the General Certificate of Education of the University of London. He continued to encourage me in my educational pursuits. His humaneness touched me to the core. It is truly unusual for people to be so well disposed and magnanimous in the face of such a challenge. I have always remained grateful for his generosity of spirit. I must add that he volunteered the statement that he had thought that nobody in that school could write that well. Was his attitude the result of the elitist thinking that existed among those who had attended the well-endowed Christian mission and government-owned schools? Like many who attended such schools, he often said that no one outside of those schools could perform well.

Interestingly, I had a similar experience while I was undergoing postgraduate studies in the United States. The only course that I had some difficulty with was statistics. I had no difficulty with the large-frame computer. I was even good at writing the programs. But I found every excuse to avoid statistics. Each time I had statistics on my study timetable, I would find myself watching television. I had to give away my television set and plead with my neighbor not to allow me to watch his television to pass my statistics course. But I was good in every other course. I had good grades except for one two-semester course in psychological assessment. It required the administration and analysis of psychological instruments and presentation of reports on patients, both young and old. I thought I was pretty good in this class, but a young lecturer fresh from the University of Minnesota thought differently. I could only earn C or D grades on his papers. I did not believe they were my actual grades.

A colleague of mine, who I will call Mark, was a guru in statistics and gave me assistance. He had no skills in clinical assessment, however, so I assisted him with that subject. (Later, he had to leave the program, precisely because he failed clinical assessment.) Mark was clumsy with patients, especially children. I not only assisted him with the administration of tests but often, after joint evaluation and discussion of the test protocols, prepared both our reports myself. His wife, Patricia, would type the reports for us. When the papers were graded, Mark would get an A or B, while I would receive a C or D. I had to report the matter to my major supervisors. Mark was himself uncomfortable with what was happening and encouraged me in my protest. Unknown to the teacher, I was asked to bring my next (handwritten) report to the head of the department and his team. After they evaluated the handwritten report, I then had the report typed and submitted to the teacher. When the reports were graded, the teacher awarded Mark an A, and I had a D!

The erring teacher was called to order. He acknowledged his bias. He confessed that he didn't believe that anyone from Africa could produce such good psychological reports, and that he'd assumed that someone else wrote the reports for me. He'd graded the papers even before he read them, or perhaps he never even read my papers. I might have been quick to shout "racism!" but, was it? I recalled my experience at Metropolitan College, Onitsha, where the teacher did not believe that anyone in that school could write the essays I wrote. It seemed to me that bias as an outcrop of elitism or racism is an ever-present and unfortunate feature of human interactions. I later became good friends with the young assistant professor and when he lost his job at the university, he asked me to help him obtain a position at Miami Dade County Psychological Services, where I worked. Ironically, he lost his job because he did not send out his papers to scholarly journals for publication, although he was quite a good researcher. He had a fear of being found inadequate by journal reviewers, a fear of being criticized. Reportedly, some of his students recognized this, and sent off one of his research papers under a pseudonym. It was published with very minor corrections. How about that!

I encountered the same problem of prejudice/bias during my pre-doctoral clinical internship at a psychiatric institute in Philadelphia. I had a twelve- to thirteen-month internship, and there were two other clinical psychology interns—a young man I will call Dick and a pretty young lady named Cory de Torres de Chonolsky, a romantic, fanciful name that did fit her beauty and her exquisite lady poise. Her bearing was aristocratic (although I never asked if she were), but she was not snobbish. On the contrary, she was a very warm and gracious person.

At the institute, interns were rated according to their training reports, and I was ranked number one among the three of us. I had no idea how the training reports were actually used in the rating. I had no way of verifying the information. Anyway, I enjoyed my stay there; receiving excellent training and honing my clinical skills, but it was not without interesting incidents.

The director of the psychology clinic, Dr. Jack Lit, was a wonderful man who gave the interns every encouragement and exposure. After one clinic conference, I came to my table the next day to find the file of a patient who had been assigned to me. I was delighted. The interns were always looking for new challenging cases and were eager to get assignments. When I opened the case file, however, I saw to my dismay that the case was that of a young Caucasian man who was a homosexual. My heart began to pound, and my pulse went into overdrive. The case had been discussed at the conference the previous day, but it didn't occur to me that it could be assigned to me. I had no previous experience in working with gay people, and I truly panicked. I rushed to Dr. Lit's office clutching the case file and said to him, perhaps not too coherently, "I saw this case."

Dr. Lit looked at me with a twinkle in his eyes and said, "And so?" I sat down, speechless. He was obviously aware of my discomfort and clearly had anticipated my reaction. After a while, he said in his gentle voice, "I saw how distressed and uncomfortable you were yesterday during the discussions on this case. It is obvious you are personally uncomfortable with this group of patients. That's why you must work with this patient to help you with your own discomfort. I know you have good clinical skills and will do well with him."

I was not comforted by Dr. Lit's glowing appraisal of my skills. Still, I booked the appointment to see the young man. I had to. I didn't have much of a choice. The days before the young man was due to come were nightmarish for me. I read up on clinical approaches to special client groups and listened to audio taped therapy sessions. In addition to the extensive, in-house, pre-session supervision I received, I also held discussions with a seasoned psychologist in private practice, a man who had extensive experience in the area. He recommended a book called *Changing Homosexuality in the Male: Treatment of Men Troubled by Homosexuality* by Dr. Lawrence Hatterer, a detail-filled tome of about 480 pages, which I read and re-read three times within a period of one week. I was that desperate!

When the young man (let us call him Tom) came, I still had no idea how to comport myself. I felt awkward. He was handsome and a bit on the portly side. I hoped he would not notice my discomfort. He may have. Clients have a way of seeing through the façade of clinicians when there is dissimulation or unease. In any case, I had to listen to his difficulties. He said, "I am teaching at a primary school and am so scared they might find out that I am gay and have me sacked."

The gay rights movement was still feeble and had not yet acquired the strong advocacy that now prevails. Tom had a nagging conflict and unease over his sexual orientation. He was intensely troubled that his parents and siblings did not know that he was gay. He said his mother was always trying to foist girls on him and did not understand his indifference. On the interpersonal level, he was having difficulties with his lover, Fred. Looking extremely distressed, he said, "Fred is always telling me that I am fat. He complains about my cooking, and he doesn't pick me up at the subway or bus stop as he used to. He tells me to find my way. He didn't use to do that before. Besides, he is not fond of my cat. He is always kicking Ruby [the cat], which makes me so sad."

Tom was also worried that Fred was seeing some other lover on the side. In a mournful tone, he said, "I'm sure he is seeing another guy; his clothes smell different now." Tom hadn't been getting much sleep, and he was very depressed, with episodes of auditory hallucination, (that is, hearing voices that are not really there). His ability to concentrate was seriously compromised, and this was affecting his ability to teach.

In the initial phase of contact, I confess I was taken aback by the content of discourse, particularly his role in the relationship, and the intensity of emotions, especially because this was a man expressing such deep sensual emotions for another man. Reading about and discussing homosexuality was one thing; coming face to face in this intimate encounter was something else, considering the ultra-traditional background of my upbringing.

Thanks to the good clinical background I'd received, the clinician in me soon took over (thanks to my teachers at the University of Miami and my clinical supervisors in Philadelphia. The University of Miami had and still has an excellent program with an outstanding group of international scholars). I was able to listen with the third ear (a depth of understanding beyond mere auditory awareness), and appreciate that sitting on the couch before me was a human being with a problem, period. Very soon, we established a good therapy relationship, with increasing resolution of his conflicts and mine too, I imagine, thanks to Dr. Lit. I certainly became comfortable with him and other categories of patients with whom I previously might have experienced some discomfort or felt unable to handle. During the therapeutic process, Tom found more satisfying employment, a lucrative sales position, and achieved a healthy state of mind. Dr. Lit commended me during a clinic conference for the young man's successful therapy outcome. At the point of formal termination of therapy, my client and I had a warm relationship. We hugged before he departed, and he kept in touch with me long after I'd left Philadelphia.

One of my supervisors in the area of child and adolescent psychiatry (let us call her Dr. Noble) had no interest in working with me. She would assign to me only retarded black children, cases that did not appear to offer much challenge in terms of therapy skills. One day, Dr. Noble called me to her office and announced that she was assigning me a rather challenging case. I was excited. I guess that I was so excited that I went to the bathroom. When I came back, I found my colleague Dick celebrating because the same case had been assigned to him! I was hurt and angry. My spontaneous reaction was to ask the clinic secretary, Jeanne Leach, whose office was directly opposite mine, to send for Dr. Noble, to tell her that I wanted to see her in my office. Imagine the nerve of me asking my supervisor to come to my office. But that was the extent of my anger and frustration. I had had enough! I also asked Dick to join us. I didn't bother to tell him why.

Dr. Noble came. I stood up, looked her straight in the face, eyeball to eyeball, and with my right fingers pointing to my other hand, I said, "Is the color of my skin the reason why I am not getting good cases from you, even though I am told I am the number one intern? You have just assigned the case you promised me to Dick. Why?"

Dr. Noble sat down, fumbled in her bag, asked for a drink, took out a tablet, and swallowed it. After a long pause, she said, "Felix, I am sorry. Do take the case, please." She followed this with several apologies and Dick also appealed to me to take the case. I accepted.

Seeing the contriteness expressed by Dr. Noble, I apologized to her for the apparent harshness of my reaction (whether or not it was warranted) and especially for playing the racial card. We had very good relationship from then on. She became completely forthcoming in her supervision and I learned quite a lot from her. She was a skilled clinician and in my estimation, a truly noble person. Outside of our contrived social shells and masks, humans can be truly human. Later on, one of her relatives attempted suicide by jumping into a pool, and she called me in for consultations over the psychotherapy treatment options. Dr. Noble was by then full of praise for my clinical skills. One day, in the context of our new, warm and frank relationship, she said, "You know, Felix, something in me had refused to accept that someone with your background could be as good as you were billed to be."

Well, that something was prejudice, pure and simple. Dr. Lit referred to this matter during the wonderful send-off they gave the interns. He said, "One thing I like about Felix is that he handles his problems himself. He never came whining or complaining about anything. As an example, he and Dr. Noble sorted out their problems without telling me. I merely heard of it later from other sources."

Prejudice, whether from elitism or racism or religion or other sources, permeates all sorts of life circumstances. All it takes is one small, perceived difference or circumstance between individuals or groups, even within a family setting, for prejudice to arise. I suppose that the problems of racial and religious prejudice evoke more ire because of their fundamental connection to matters of equity and justice, and the accompanying denial of rights to targeted populations. My attitude is that when people get to know each other and deal with each other on a one-to-one basis rather than due to some classification or pre-conceived notion, the walls of prejudice off whatever hue usually crumble. In the final analysis, it appears that the meaningful response is always to confront all forms of prejudice squarely and force the offending individuals or groups to recognize that their actions or attitudes are improper and unacceptable.

Chapter 14

The War Years and Diplomatic Service

It was 1967, the year that the Nigerian Civil War started; it would not end until 1970. In the face of ethnic killings of thousands of easterners, especially Igbo people, in the north of the country, the Eastern Region of Nigeria declared itself the Republic of Biafra and held on to its sovereignty for three years. As with most conflicts, there were multiple causes, including ethnic rivalries, social inequities and perceived injustices, cultural and religious differences, among others. It was, in part, the sheer problems of evolving functional cohesion of formerly diverse peoples into nation states in the post-colonial era. The colonial powers created countries, without regard for the homogeneity or lack of homogeneity of the populace. The Nigeria-Biafra conflict was a brutal war, resulting in millions of deaths due to acts of war, hunger caused by territorial blockade, and disease. As with many human disasters and tragedies, the memory of this horrific war is now largely forgotten in international discourse.

We were living in Enugu in eastern Nigeria at the time. We had four living children. My graduation at the University of Nigeria in June was a rushed and evening affair. War was in the air. The wounded and dead were brought down in droves to Enugu from the north via railway. The radio airwaves were crowded with rhetoric and threats of conflict. Suddenly, the war was on. We had to evacuate Enugu in a hurry. Told that the move was temporary, I left Enugu with only a briefcase and documents and certificates that I could easily find. Other documents that were lodged in a bank remained there and were eventually lost. Susan and the children went to Onitsha and then on to Atani. I moved on through Awka to Umuahia, the new headquarters of the

Biafran government, to report for duty. Awka was the beginning of the harsh experiences of war for me and for many who passed through the town. The inhabitants of that ancient town called everybody who was hanging around or passing through, saboteurs! We were told that we had sold out in Enugu and now were planning to invade Awka and bring the federal troops there.

Getting accommodation in Umuahia was very difficult. I had to share one tiny room with five other young men, sometimes even six or seven. We slept like sardines, stretched out in a row. But lady luck was to come our way. Nearly opposite lived this old man, the landlord of the multi-story building he occupied. His name was Mr. Okonkwo. We played draughts (checkers) most evenings, if there were no air raids by the Nigerian Air Force. The game is a funny one. There is usually a lot of banter, with insults intertwined with pleasantries coming from the two players, and sometimes even the watching enthusiasts participated in the taunting and teasing. I am not sure that there is any other game in which abusive teasing is so much part of the game's culture. One day, the old man and I were at play. Disregarding the age difference, we taunted, teased, and abused each other without letting up. He said to me, "You little boy, if you live to be a hundred, your intelligence will not be enough to beat me. Your brain is full of cotton wool. There is no single gray matter in your head!"

When he showed some hesitation in making a move, I taunted him also, saying, "Your old age is dealing with you! You are becoming senile. You wasted your entire life energy in the excessive number of children you were busy fathering! Couldn't you find some other recreation?"

One fateful day while some banter was going on, he looked at me and said, "You open-toothed boy," referring to the gap in my front teeth, "where are you from? Where is your home town?"

I asked him what my teeth and town had to do with the game, or was he afraid to play and stalling for time. He retorted, "I can see that you are ashamed of your hometown."

After a while, I told him that I was from Atani in Ogbaru, along the riverbanks near Onitsha. He repeated the word "Atani" and then said something significant, "You won't know him, but that is the hometown of a dear friend of mine, Dominic Onedibie, who died too early."

Curious, I held my breath. "What," I asked, "was your business with him?"

He told me that Dominic had helped him in business when he traded with the United Africa Company, where Dominic was in charge. Over the next week, I plied him with questions about Dominic to make sure that their relationship was indeed cordial and pleasant. He knew the family well.

When I was satisfied that they indeed had the good relationship he claimed, I asked him:

"This Dominic, wasn't his full name Dominic Odili Onedibie?" "

He said, "Yes," looking quite surprised.

Again I went on, "Did he imprint the letters 'D.O.O' on his cutlery, spoons, and forks?"

He said "Yes," and asked, "How do you know this? You are too young to know him."

I wouldn't have told him that Dominic was my father if they were enemies! But feeling safe enough regarding their relationship, I said, "He is my father."

He shouted, "Yes! That's where you got your open teeth. He must be your father. I have always felt there was something about your face." His next question was interesting. In Igbo, he said, "I na ma kwa akukwo ka nna yi?" (Are you brilliant, good in school like your father?) And then, "What about your mother, that beautiful woman?"

I told him my mother was fine and that I had just completed my university education. He told me that what we did then was not education, that education during his and my father's time was the real education. He asked if my handwriting was as good as my father's. I said no, which was true. My father's writing seemed as if a lithographic machine printed the letters. The old man said, "There you are."

From then on, if I beat him at draughts, he would say that he felt he was playing with my father. After this, I could not do any more serious banter with him. I watched my words as I played the game because I was playing with someone who was my father's contemporary, someone who, in fact, knew my father very well. The game with him became a dull affair because I could not add the juice that gives the game of draughts its flavor—the bragging, teasing, and taunting. Because I had lived away from my family, I learned a lot from this grand old man about my father's disposition.

After he became aware of who I was, the old man took one look at me and said, "Are you not one of the rascals living over there?" He was pointing at a house nearly opposite. I said "yes," not minding the rascal bit. After all, abuse was and remains part of the draughts culture. And, in the context of our new relationship as my father's friend and contemporary, he could indeed call me anything. He said, "You will move into two rooms in my house. Dominic's son will live in my house so I can repay him for what he did for me."

He ordered a young man to vacate one of the rooms and move upstairs and insisted that I move into two of the rooms downstairs. Knowing the difficulties of accommodation at the time, with a war raging, I sought to take only one room. I had no furniture to put into an additional room. All one needed during the war was sleeping space and a mat. But he insisted that I take the two rooms, and I also enjoyed the additional luxury of a bamboo bed that he provided and, many times, meals from his kitchen. I asked him half in jest and half seriously if some of my "rascal" friends could move in with me. He said yes. A couple of the young men did so.

That's how my accommodation problem in Umuahia was solved. In addition, I got myself a grand old man for a dear friend. He often gave me food gifts to deliver to my family, who had then moved from Atani to take refuge with a dear friend of ours, Lawrence Onyeagoro, at Emohe, near Emekuku in what is now Imo State. I inherited my father's friend. My loss was that I couldn't tease and taunt him during draughts games as I used to. I had to watch my language when we played. Not too long after, I joined the Biafran Foreign Service and traveled out of the country, but he retained my accommodation for me with no rent payment. (Well, Dad was paying my rent from beyond the grave!) On one trip back to Biafra for consultations, I brought him gifts of clothes and cigarettes, which were good currency for getting other needed items. When I came back to Nigeria in 1976 to bury my son Arinzechukwu, I took a special trip to Umuahia to see him only to find that the grand and gentle old man, my friend, had just passed away.

Shortly after I arrived in Umuahia in 1967, Dr. Kalu Aja, my erstwhile lecturer at the University of Nigeria, established what he called a retraining military corps at Abiriba, some thirty minutes ride from Umuahia, which had become the new Biafran capital. Dr. Aja brought a number of psychology graduates to work with him. Our tasks involved interviewing and retraining straggler soldiers, the wounded and convalescing, and those who had become disillusioned with the war. We interviewed them, gave them motivating lectures, including one-to-one interactions; and encouraged their early return to combat or to any other duties for which they were fit. I was released by my ministry to become involved in this assignment. We had some military training, and we were assigned ranks and issued uniforms. It was on return from one of the trips to Abiriba that I received a paper that looked like an old-time telegram, directing me to report to the Foreign Ministry for assignment. That was to presage a great change in my life.

I have never been able to ascertain why and how I was appointed to the Foreign Ministry. I did not apply, either verbally or in writing, and I had no discussion with anyone about moving from the Ministry of Agriculture to the Ministry of Foreign Affairs. The posting came as a total surprise. All I can imagine is that I maintained a record of working hard at my assignments and postings; perhaps my records spoke for me as they did when I was posted from Owerri to Enugu, ahead of other colleagues, to take on a significant assignment. Those were the days when merit was the preeminent consideration in the public service, not as was the case after the war, with ethnic and political considerations holding sway. On reflection, I also have a sneaky suspicion that the head of the Foreign Ministry, Ambassador Godwin Onyegbula, had a hand in this. He often stated that he sought to assemble a corps of young bright people who he referred to as "the ministry's whiz kids." Many young and fresh university graduates thus were employed directly, or moved from their primary ministries, to the Ministry of Foreign Affairs. Edna Akwiwu, Cyril Nwanunobi, Basil Nwozuzu, and many others were part of this deployment. Most of us had first-class honors degrees. Ambassador Onyegbula often challenged us to come up with options for action regarding Biafra's diplomatic engagements.

At the Foreign Ministry, we underwent some training, and I was assigned to work with the team focused on Latin America and the Caribbean States. Our assignment was to establish relationships and seek recognition from the nations in that hemisphere. The team I worked with was composed of Okechukwu Ikejiani, a well-known medical doctor with outstanding national political experience, who was team leader, and Kalu Ezera, a distinguished professor of political science. Both were men of outstanding intellect and full of ideas. They were opposites in temperament but complemented each other wonderfully. Dr. Ikejiani was calm and calculating, always puffing on his pipe while contemplating issues. He usually sought everyone's contribution before arriving at a decision. On the other hand, Professor Ezera was forceful and impatient for action. Dr. Ikejiani was especially interesting to watch. He didn't need much regular sleep and lived on catnaps. He would catnap for five minutes and wake up totally refreshed, able to continue with interminable hours of engagement. It was truly amazing. I was the administrative man on the team, which would be joined in the United States by Chukwuma Azikiwe for the trip to the Republic of Haiti only. Chukwuma Azikiwe was the eldest son of the Right Honorable Dr. Nnamdi Azikiwe, one of the nationalists who fought for the independence of Nigeria. I learned later that his inclusion on the team was because the then ruler of Haiti, Dr. François Duvallier (nicknamed Papa Doc), and Nnamdi Azikiwe were classmates. Ours was, in my view, a well-constituted team.

When I was invited to the Foreign Service position, I was troubled. I did not want to leave my family, and I said so, loud enough for the authorities to hear. I asked when they would allow my wife and children to join me if I accepted the posting. There was no meaningful response. One of the senior personnel called me to his office and said in Igbo, "O ife ne me unu bu ndi Ogbaru, ndi mmili, Ule. Nkaa bu ife ndi ozo na yo ayo ka enyelu gi, i ne fe isi." (This is what is wrong with you people from Ogbaru, laidback, lazy riverine people. This offer is what others are begging for, and it comes to you, and you are not appreciative.)

I honestly did not feel appreciative. He was right about Ogbaru people being laidback, but we certainly are not lazy. There is a huge difference between being laidback and being lazy. I said to myself that he should go and do the backbreaking yam farming that is the Ogbaru lifestyle or spend whole nights in the river, fishing and casting very heavy nets. Then he would know what hard work really is, that it was much different from his sedentary desk job! Lazy, certainly not, but laidback—that probably was true. Ogbaru people, by their culture, are not as intensely driven as some of their neighbors and do not seek the attainment of goals at all cost as is the attitude among some other people. Ogbaru people have a more leisurely attitude toward life and are less inclined to excessive pursuit of material things. Indeed, Ogbaru culture was pristine. Hard work was an overarching ideal and, even today, the people have songs that despise those who are idle. Truthfulness and caring about family and neighbors were guiding principles in their social life, always with the goal of protecting the family name. Of course, as I write, it is obvious that all Nigerian cultures are now in dynamic flux, and changes, good and bad, are becoming apparent all over.

The truth is that I did not want to leave my family—wife, children, mother, brothers and sisters, uncles and aunts, the entire family— in Biafra, with the war raging and all the hunger and uncertainty. I wanted to be around to assist my family in those troubled times. I believed I could opt out of the posting because I knew of one young man who pleaded ill health and had his posting cancelled; he was assigned to a desk job at headquarters. I went to the village and talked to Uncle Luke about the offer. Surprisingly, he was delighted, and so were my wife and brothers. Only my mother, always worrying, demurred. We were set to go; our destinations were Haiti, Jamaica, Trinidad and Tobago, Antigua, Guyana, and Barbados for starters, with our base in the United States. Other countries would be visited when appropriate.

We had some training and spent the final preparatory days in discussions on strategy. We met with the head of state, His Excellency Colonel Chukwuemeka Odumegwu Ojukwu, who gave us further instructions and a pep talk about the importance of our mission. The ardor in his voice was palpable. He exuded vibrant confidence and a determined sense of purpose. He always spoke with calm measured deliberateness. In his presence, one felt the real weight of the task we were assigned. I was not alone in this feeling. Others who encountered him were similarly affected, including even some of his close associates who one would think would be used to him. His commitment to the defense of his people was passionate, and he communicated that passion when one was in his very intense presence. Of course, the events preceding the war were glaring; the selective killing of Igbos and some others from the south of the country in most parts of northern Nigeria was rampant. The evidence of pogrom committed against the Igbos was all over the place, in public talks; in the newspapers, with shocking photographs of maimed and dead people; and on the radio. No one needed any prodding. But it was added flame when the head of state spoke to you.

After the usual paper work and preparations, we were set to go. In the evening of the appointed date, we headed for the Biafran airstrip at Uli. Well into the night, we got into the plane. There were no regular seats. Instead, we sat on makeshift structures, including bags of produce meant for export. Seat belts, routinely touted as life preservers in regular air flights, were totally absent! As we took off, we were assailed by ground fire from the Nigerian artillery. We could hear the sounds and see the flares. It was a frightening experience. Soon we were fully airborne and on our way. We had a brief stop at São Tomé and then flew off to Portugal. It was pitch dark for most of the take-off flight. In Nigerian/Biafran airspace, the pilots dared not show lights, inside or outside the plane.

In the wee hours of the morning, we arrived Portugal. We landed at Faro Airport. I learned that we were not allowed to land at the international airport in the capital Lisbon (the Portuguese spell it Lisboa); there was one other reason for this besides the diplomatic one. During my first outing, when we got down from the plane at Faro Airport at dawn, the sight of the plane was frightening. It was old and rickety. There was hardly any paintwork on the body. Indeed, it was rusty all over, and there was oil dripping from the sides of the plane. Real *Bolekaja*. I believe the plane was a Super Constellation, an old and abandoned model that the ingenious Biafran pilots flew with considerable bravery. In fact, sometimes while in flight, we would hear the pilots saying that an engine had gone off, and they would work feverishly, fiddling with wires, to get the engine to work. Perhaps their frank and open discussion of the state of the aircraft was because we were at war. The Biafran pilots had no qualms about letting everyone know the state of the aircraft at each point in time. In commercial flights, however, the crew makes some attempt to keep nerves calm by being economical with information regarding any operational difficulties. On one flight back to Biafra, we ran on one engine for a considerable distance. One of those Super Constellation planes was lost in the Sahara with a colleague of ours on board. I had just helped him do some shopping for his family at a shopping mall in New York two days earlier. The plane was never found.

Going from Faro Airport to Lisbon was wonderful experience. Despite the long flight from Sao Tome, I kept awake throughout the bus ride. The countryside was marvelous. The vegetation was lush, and the flowers were entrancing. It was nature in exotic splendor. Women were washing clothes in community centers, similar to the communal clothes washing areas in northern Nigeria. It was a dreamlike countryside. We drove straight to the Biafran consulate, which was located at Rue Alexandre Braga 2-4B. We had good meals, such as we had not had in Biafra for some time, and then settled down to planning the trip to New York via Montreal, Canada. Lisbon was my first experience of eating without water. There was no water on the table. There was only wine. Everybody drank wine with his or her food. Water had to be specially ordered and bought. The food was good, but the absence of water made things a bit difficult for me. After complaining for a few days, the matter was remedied, and we had water at table.

We traveled on Nigerian passports and another document, the Biafran Travel Document. One of us had a diplomatic passport from a friendly country. I won't mention which country because I am not sure the involvement was ever acknowledged by that country, and I do not wish to cause unnecessary embarrassment, despite the intervening years. When we arrived in Montreal, the French-speaking immigration officials were difficult. One of our team members, Professor Ezera, made matters worse by insisting that we were British Commonwealth citizens and did not need visas to get into another Commonwealth country. The French-speaking officials took umbrage, shouting, "To hell with your Commonwealth!"

We were herded into a hotel and ordered not to step out of the front door until our case was resolved. That was my one and only imprisonment in life, so far. (Considering the state of human rights in many African countries, "so far" is the right attitude, and one must then say "knock on wood" with all fingers crossed!) But our "imprisonment" was not that bad. We had the run of the hotel, the bar, and the dance hall, which had a live band in the evenings (featuring lightly or barely dressed, delectable female dancers). We could eat whatever we wanted, and we could look out the glass panes at the traffic and neon lights outside.

Our circumstances were precarious, however. We faced repatriation. The nagging question was, would it be to Nigeria? Nigeria was a member of the Commonwealth; Biafra was not. And some of us were traveling on Nigerian passports! It took the intervention of the Catholic bishop of Montreal for the matter to be resolved and for us to be allowed to continue on our journey to the United States. In 1995, twenty-six years later, I was on a Ford Foundation–sponsored research trip to the Canadian Science Foundation in my capacity as president of the Social Science Academy of Nigeria. I thought about locating my old "jail," in Montreal, but I had forgotten the name of the hotel.

We arrived in New York at the John F. Kennedy International Airport and made straight for the Biafran Embassy at 342 Madison Avenue for briefing before we were shuttled to the Hotel Diplomat. The name of the hotel sounded highbrow to me. Since this was my first taste of diplomatic work, I thought all diplomats stayed there. I was to be disillusioned quickly. The hotel was a glorified whorehouse, a large but seedy place with girls propositioning men at every turn. But it was cheap, and I imagine that was what the struggling Biafran mission could afford. However, the Nigerian consulate held many of its parties there, a number of which I was invited to at the end of the conflict. In any case, the enthusiasm for the job and the Biafran struggle did not permit one to reflect too long on such matters. The reality of hunger and privation that one had just left behind in Biafra made any inconvenience in New York of little significance.

The Biafran Embassy was a beehive of activity, twenty-four hours a day. A variety of consultations would be going on at the same time in different rooms and even along the corridors. The telex message machine was forever busy. There were no regular work hours. A twenty-hour workday was normal. Everybody was called into service, and there were volunteers (mostly white) in the hundreds, seeking to be involved. Many foreigners were touched by the Biafran anguish and came in droves to give whatever succor and assistance they could. Their zeal and enthusiasm was tremendous. The Biafran ambassador was Dr. Nwoye Otue and his assistants were Dr Andrew Onejeme and Ralph Nwakoby. Bedford Fubara, now a professor, was part of the administrative staff and also assisted with the message machine when the operator was away.

Our team settled down, got the necessary briefings, and quickly started planning our trip. Since Chukwuma Azikiwe was to accompany us only on the trip to Haiti, that was our first port of call. Apparently some considerable diplomatic work had been done ahead of our trip, and there was strong hope that recognition of Biafra would be forthcoming from Haiti. It was reasoned that if recognition was obtained from Haiti, it would inspire the other countries on our agenda to be more forthcoming.

The trip to Haiti was interesting. The reception was wonderful. We had a red-carpet reception. We were given their Foreign Ministry's diplomatic vehicles for our engagements. We met with the Foreign Ministry officials, and an appointment was made for us to meet with the head of state two days later. In the meantime, many people and groups feted us, and we certainly felt welcome. The first thing that struck me was the name of the hotel in which we were housed. It was the Ibo lele Hotel. (The word Igbo is some times spelt as Ibo). That was something. I could not find out whether Igbo people owned the hotel.

It was interesting to discover the variety of ways in which Haitians were attached to their African roots, particularly in arts and culture. Many of the people we visited, usually in the upper and middle classes, had definite understanding of their ancestral roots, whether Igbo, Yoruba, or some other tribe in Nigeria. There also were claims of origins from Ghana as well as Benin, perhaps the whole range of the West African sub-region, perhaps beyond. The patois or Creole they spoke was difficult to understand, and the little French I had in school helped only a little. Thankfully, most of the Foreign Ministry officials were multilingual.

Meeting with President Duvallier was an experience. He was taciturn but showed considerable warmth toward Chukwuma Azikiwe, whom he referred to repeatedly as "my friend's son." We made extensive presentations about the Biafran struggle, with several Haitian diplomatic personnel participating in the dialogue that followed. President Duvallier praised the Biafran resolve. In the end, he gave us the green light regarding recognition and told us that Haiti was with Biafra in the fight for independence. As we got back to New York, the Haitian government announced the recognition of Biafra as a sovereign state. We were ecstatic about the achievement.

We had a beautiful time in Haiti. The capital, Port-au-Prince, particularly its coastline, was a delightful place to be. We were feted with diplomatic courtesies and extensive parties. The depressing part, however, was when we ventured outside the capital, to the immediate countryside. There was stark poverty. People were living in shanties, with animals all over. Donkey was the predominant mode of transportation. The contrast between the flamboyant lifestyle we were shown in the city and the stark poverty of the immediate countryside was hard to reconcile. It is no wonder that the country continues to be mired in revolutions and instability.

The trips to the other countries were pleasant. Jamaica presented an initial difficulty. There was resistance to meeting with our delegation. The prime minister was the Honorable Hugh Shearer. We were kept waiting for days, and we were running low on money. Professor Ezera was particularly peeved; he lost his temper and said we should go. I offered to see the senior men in the Ministry of Foreign Affairs and was encouraged to go. I met with them and found that there was, in fact, a ground swell of sympathy for the Biafran cause, but that one official was in the way. After discussions with him, the matter was resolved, and we were immediately invited to meet with the head of state. Subsequently, we were helped to seek funds from various organizations in Jamaica, and we were given the go-ahead to raise our issues in the Jamaican press. We had quite a lot of coverage, including interviews with the *Jamaican Gleaner* and other media. When we were in Jamaica, an airline strike took place. But we had garnered such sufficient goodwill with the officials that they arranged for us to use flight facilities that usually were strictly available to special personnel only.

The trips to British Guyana, Trinidad and Tobago, Barbados, and Antigua were equally fruitful, but we achieved only tentative leanings toward Biafra. One sensed that these governments were sitting on the fence, waiting for the outcome of the conflict before determining their final positions. They were generally supportive, however, and allowed us free access to their media for airing the Biafran point of view, including live interviews. Two significant constraints on the West Indian governments were (a) their relationship with Britain—while we were in one country, the prime minister was accorded the queen's honor—and (b) their routine stance against balkanization, that is, the break up of nations into smaller units. These were people who were excited about their African origins and were sold on the inspiring image of one united Africa, promoted by African leaders like Kwame Nkrumah of Ghana, Nnamdi Azikiwe of Nigeria, Leopold Senghor of Senegal, and others. They were fired up with the dream of an all-embracing African nation and any suggestion of some territorial break was difficult for them to understand, even when they appreciated that the humanitarian and security imperatives in the conflict demanded action. Biafra also suffered from the international politics of oil, but that's another story.

West Indian people are wonderful people, full of vitality and life, and fun loving. It is no surprise that they gave the world calypso and reggae. During our tours, we took in a couple of the annual carnivals in Barbados and Antigua. The one in Antigua was especially fascinating, with street-long floats, fascinating color displays, massive masquerades, and, of course, titillating Caribbean sounds, including the calypso. It was my first direct sight of the West Indian steel drums, and I saw for myself the sound source of the calypsos.

Caribbean social life was leisurely. We took boat rides from Trinidad to Tobago. And the scenery was wonderful. The hotels on the beachfronts where we stayed were strategically located for maximum entertainment. In one of the hotels, your feet could touch the water while you took your meal. The hotel restaurant and rest area was built as a projection onto the waterfront at a low enough gradient to allow for close contact with water with hands or feet but with spaced protective steel bars as base. Beyond the hotel enclave, there was the beachfront for walks along tree-lined shores. And all the while, there would be popular songs assailing one gently from various directions, cool and pleasing. I am amazed that the songs I recorded on cassettes from a radio station in Barbados in 1969, almost forty years ago, still play fairly well even today. One of them, *Three Coins in a Fountain*, remains one of my all time favorites.

Guyana was different from the islands; it was somewhat staid, with a strong presence of the old colonial ways. Stiff, or maybe stuffy, was my overall impression. At our hotel, the female secretary we employed was not allowed to work in any of our rooms! These were real colonial pretensions about morality. Incidentally, in Guyana, I threatened to leave the Foreign Service. While in the capital, Georgetown, we received news that the market in Atani had been strafed by the Nigerian Air Force and that many people had died. I sent word to the ministry of my distress over the news and requested that I be recalled. The head of the Foreign Ministry, Ambassador Onyegbula, went to Atani himself, saw my family, and sent a message informing me that the news was exaggerated and only one person had been killed during the bombing. My family was safe. He urged me to continue with my assignment. He also informed Susan that I was hale and hearty. That's how caring and humane this great man is, to give his very limited time to ease the personal distress of a junior staff member.

The West Indies is truly fascinating, with so much of nature's allure and peopled by a warm hospitable people. Caribbean food is delicious, especially the Haitian equivalent of the Nigerian *jollof* rice, curried, spicy and creamy, truly a gourmet's delight. The speech variations in the islands were pleasing to note. The Trinidadian sentence sound is songlike, going up and down in undulating tonal variations, while the Jamaican rendering is much like the regular Rastafarian speech sound familiar to the world. They all took some getting used to. I have continued to wish I could get back to the islands, mostly to feed my nostalgia. A few times during my stay in Florida, I nearly hopped over but missed the opportunities. Someday, I will.

Between designated trips, I was permanently assigned as staff of the New York embassy, with coverage portfolios that included the West Indies, Latin America, the United States, and Canada. There was fundraising to do; there were various groups to canvass, and reports to prepare. As a major part of my assignment, I was required to prepare separate confidential situation reports to home office, distinct from the reports submitted by my team. Perhaps this was intended as a check on the reporting of the political appointees who might embellish their reports unduly. There was really a lot of work to do, and traveling too. I was in this role when the war suddenly ended.

The day the war ended was a mournful day at the embassy. It was also the day our work at the embassy terminated. Nobody was in the mood to talk. Anguish was written over all of our faces, including those of the foreign people who were supporting the cause, black and white alike. For a while, a sense of doom and gloom prevailed, especially because the fate of the head of state, Colonel Odumegwu Ojukwu was not immediately known. There was a strong rumor that he had been beheaded in a public place. That was hard to take. The gloom was lifted somewhat when we learned that he was alive and had taken up residence in Ivory Coast. That provided some psychological lift and a lesser sense of loss. From then on, it was "To your tents, oh Israel," and without much ado, each person took his or her fate in his or her own hands. The embassy could not afford even the next month's rent for the staff. However, the office remained open for some time, and we gathered around to seek news from home, commiserate with one another, and support each other in the search for survival options.

Generally, my experience of diplomatic life was rewarding due to the direct contact with heads of state and functionaries, with the media and, of course, because of the various social encounters, which provided added enlightenment. There was so much to learn, about people and about governments. However, I found some incidents at the Biafran embassy quite painful. One was the "Club 250" affair. A well-known Biafran big shot came to the United States and promoted the idea of a Club 250. It involved the payment of $250 by all Biafran nationals in the United States. This was intended to raise funds to support the war effort and a lot of enthusiasm went into the drive for this venture. The embassy assisted in coordinating the drive. Money flowed in. There was incredible goodwill among the Biafran people, Igbos and non-Igbos alike. Foreigners donated most generously. When so much of the money had come in, the big man collected the bulk of the proceeds and made away with it; to our understanding, he never released the money for the war effort and rejected all appeals made to him. Most of us were disillusioned by this event. It was a low point at the embassy.

Another event was a personal one. One significant Biafran operative urged me to get into a deal with him to set up a taxi company in London. He had done, he said, the initial feasibility studies and insisted that the enterprise promised great financial rewards. He reasoned that Biafra was already a success; what was at issue was who would be the first group of millionaires in Biafra. He urged me, as the administrative man on our team and responsible for the accounting, to fix the travel accounts to garner funds. He showed me how we could report expenses so that expenditures in Jamaica with a lower currency value, for example, could be reflected as the American dollar equivalent, with the difference coming to us. He also urged me to divert some of the donations I received from people and organizations during my various tours to the planned taxi company project. He told me that other people were lining their pockets in that manner. I asked him where his parents and family were. He said they were in Biafra, right in the middle of the war zone. I looked him in the face and told him to get lost or maybe something worse, said in the heat of my temper, but I will spare the reader such untidy language.

During the war, a couple of people were able to build or purchase expensive houses in Yonkers, an exclusive suburb of New York City. We all knew that their legitimate incomes did not give them sufficient money to acquire these homes. They lived in unabashed luxury during and after the conflict. Outside of Biafra, a number of officials and politicians became overwhelmed by personal greed and lost their patriotism for the cause they were sent to canvass and promote. Reflection on the state of affairs in Biafra, with young men in trenches and having only one or two bullets to fight with and often no meals to eat, made these treacherous acts very painful indeed. One Biafran leader who deserves special mention is Dr. Akanu Ibiam, the former governor of Eastern Nigeria. He accounted for every penny he garnered on his tours, with details and all particulars of the donors, and asked his staff to send appropriate acknowledgement letters. And he would also ask to be housed in the least expensive hotel. Some of the other politicians sometimes made jokes over Dr. Ibiam's transparent and almost proverbial honesty.

Unfortunately, I was persuaded to destroy my memorabilia and Biafran documents because family and friends believed that the documents would constitute danger to myself if they were brought back into Nigeria after the conflict. The brutal and savage murder of Kalu Ezera following his return to Nigeria was frequently pointed to as a reason for me to be cautious. Just like losing significant property when we left Enugu, the destruction of these documents and other items, including my father's photographs, is regrettable. Some of the documents would have certainly provided relevant documentation for this book as well as made worthwhile reference items for historians. I deposited various books on the war, as well as autographed copies of books by heads of states, including Dr. Duvallier, in the library at the University of Miami, but I never knew if they were preserved and put into circulation.

The topic of Biafra remains a real commentary on the problems of emerging states of Africa, including the issues of leadership, ethnicity, and the dynamics of welding diverse colonial peoples into nation states as well as the intrusive, obnoxious, and retrogressive influence of colonial and external constraints on evolving African nations.

Chapter 15

Wives on Auction

During the Nigerian Civil War, many young men from Biafra who were overseas and desired to marry girls from their Igbo village kindred, were unable to get home to marry. The travel process was tedious and unreliable; in addition, there were the risks of traveling in a war zone. Someone conceived the idea that Igbo girls should be encouraged to go out of the country to be chosen as wives. No one can now say what actually motivated these young people to accept such an uncertain assignment. Perhaps the harshness of the war, the excitement of going overseas, or a combination of these or other reasons were at play. We may never know. Other girls were sent for by young men who were then resident in America or Europe, having arranged that the girls would come from their own villages. Usually, the young men sent their photographs home as a means of introduction. These two categories of wives-to-be were interesting and produced mixed results. There were several deposit sites, Lisbon in Portugal, Libreville in Gabon, Sao Tome, and maybe other places. A few of these arranged marriages were successful in the short or long run, but many had serious problems.

The young men would arrive and move freely among the girls. Sometimes, the attention of a young man would be drawn to one or two girls specifically. The girls knew they were on display, and I imagine they were usually on their best behavior and appearance, to enhance their chances of being chosen. Two cases will illustrate the drama of these contrived human encounters. One young man chose one of the husband-seeking young girls in Lisbon. They went to New York and within one month, the young lady dumped the Biafran young man and took up with a black American man. All efforts and intervention to get her to stick to her earlier suitor failed. The young man was aghast and became disordered mentally. In fact, his was only one case among several others of girls who, reportedly, abandoned the men who chose them and opted for different men. It was rumored that the trend was for Biafran men in America who were seeking wives, to seduce new wives-to-be from their original suitors.

Another interesting case was one of a young man (let's call him Stanley) who sent his photograph home and persuaded a young lady (I'll call her Linda) from his village to agree to marry him. However, the photograph he sent home was one taken when he was younger and had a slim build. In the intervening years, Stanley, an accountancy graduate with a comfortable income, had grown a protruding midline pouch. He was a guy with incredible good humor. He kept asking, "How do I cover this pouch, this pregnancy?" He made himself Mao Tse-tung suits (also called Biafran suits), sufficiently wide in the attempt to cover some of his ample frontal girth. They did not work very well. The bulge was prominently easy to see.

On the day of the bride-to-be's arrival, some of us at the Biafran embassy trooped to the airport to receive her. When Linda arrived at the reception arena, she was obviously anxious to identify her husband-to-be. She looked around and asked rather simply in Igbo, "Onye ka obu?" (Who is it?) There were so many people around. Stanley stepped forward and announced himself with some flourish. Linda took a good look at him and said, "I won't even get into the same car with him, let alone marry him! He sent me a false photograph. He lied to me." Shaking her head vigorously from side to side, she kept saying in Igbo, "E kwerom, e kwerom, Mmu na Onyea? O'nwedii!" (I refuse, I refuse. Me and this person? It won't happen!)

She sounded hysterical and defiant. I could have imagined it, but it seemed to me that she was looking at Stanley's bulging middle while she was talking. We had problem on our hands. Everybody looked at everybody else. Stanley launched into a series of quips and jokes but the clearly disconcerted and distressed lady was not impressed. In the end, a man whose wife was with him persuaded her to go to his home. The quandary continued for weeks. Efforts were made by many of us and the Catholic clergy to persuade Linda to marry; they all failed. Linda continued to stay with her adoptive family. Stanley got into the habit of visiting the home every evening and became more or less a permanent fixture there. His humor was endless. You couldn't stay around him and feel sad. Stanley quipped about any and everything, and he had no reverence even for himself. Indeed, his funniest jokes were about himself. He called his bulging stomach an "advanced pregnancy," said that he knew he was about to deliver, and that with the delivery they would have their first son, and then get married, with their son being the page boy. He sent flowers by courier in the mornings and took more flowers in the evenings. He brought an endless array of gifts. Initially, Linda would not even come out into the living room to see him.

Before long, however, Stanley's jokes took effect, like some anesthetic. Linda later said, "I would stay in the room cracking up on his jokes, that foolish man, but too shy to come out." After about three months, the magic worked. Linda came out of the room, and in two weeks they were married. It was truly a festive marriage, with Stanley's jokes cracking everyone up. He had the incredible ability of making a laughter-inducing joke out of everything. He seemed always in touch with the funny side of life. Their wedding was a joyful event for all of us, a beautiful ending to a tortuous courtship.

In 1975, when I took my family to see the Statue of Liberty in New York, I visited them at their Brooklyn home. I believe they already had two children. I teased Linda, saying, "I remember one young lady at an airport lobby shouting, 'I refuse, I refuse. Me and this person? It won't happen.' Well, well, it did happen, didn't it, Mrs. Stanley?"

Linda laughed and said, "You are one of the people I have to thank for persuading me to marry this foolish man. You live with this man for one year, and there is never a dull moment. He makes you laugh, even at the most incongruous of times. He is so full of joy and his joyfulness is infectious. He should really be on TV. And look at him. He has lost his 'pregnancy' with exercise and proper eating."

She had acquired Stanley's flippant and jesting disposition. Not to be outdone, Stanley added his own quip, saying, "She has made me fit enough to now marry my real heart's desire, a proper wife, not one sent by post."

I went away, happy at the turn of events for this truly happy couple, a union that started with uncertainties and blossomed into fascinating harmony. The marriage had become a union of hearts, of two people who enjoyed each other's presence well beyond the physical. So many more of these contrived Biafran marriages did not turn out well. They must be among the tragedies of a tragic war, perhaps all wars, in which life events lose their normalcy and spontaneity, and humans must contrive ways to continue their biological, social, and psychological existence.

Chapter 16

Overseas Study and University Teaching Career: The Beginnings

Teaching was not a career that I'd sought. I had done a brief stint as a teacher of English in a small set-up in Onitsha, a place called Hope Rising Institute. That was for about three months in 1954 before I sought a position in the civil service in Enugu. My dream was to be an administrator and the ultimate position then was that of permanent secretary. The plight of teachers in public life was glaring, and I did not see myself in that profession. So, when I took up the position of assistant secretary (Foreign Service), it was still in the direction of my chosen life career. I found the process of decision-making in the civil service very interesting. Most of the young administrative officers reveled in being able to provide the necessary background information and logic that would aid the decisions of upper management. It was called "minuting." It involved arguing a case with the relevant facts so that top management could make a decision based on the logic of the presentation. Whenever someone's minute (argument) formed the core of an approved decision, it was celebrated.

My dream of a life of administrative work remained alive until the Biafran war ended suddenly in 1970, and I was stuck in the Biafran embassy in New York. I tried to go back home, but the people there would hear none of that. There was fear of reprisals, especially for those of us who had openly participated in the war effort, even if in purely administrative roles. It did not help that Kalu Ezera, a member of my diplomatic team, had been brutally murdered on his journey to his hometown Ohafia in Abia State. So, I was stuck in New York, with no money or resources.

I had forged a friendship with another embassy staff member, Bedford

Fubara, and we decided to rent a place together at 605 West End Avenue and to find employment. Bedford found one first, and then I found one at Alexander's Incorporated, a department store. I was appointed stockmen supervisor. I remember Bedford's advice for getting the job. At that time, we both smoked pipes. He advised me to make my pipe conspicuous during the interview, a ridiculous gimmick. The original advertisement had been for a lower-level job, stockman, and we agreed I should go and flaunt my credentials, including my Foreign Service record and ask if there was another job of a higher status. I did just that, and it worked! Instead of being appointed a stockman, responsible for carting goods, especially suits and other clothing, all over the floors of the stores, I was appointed a supervisor in charge of a number of workers. The only thing was that I could not smoke my pipe while working, as if that was an issue. The interviewer went to great pains to let me know that the injunction was because of fire hazards. I was not a serious smoker. My smoking was just "for show," and I needed the job badly, anyway. I had a good time working at Alexander's. Being on staff, I was able to buy very good suits at giveaway prices. When I planned to leave to go to school, they did not want to let me go. I had to pretend that I was leaving the country. The reason was that I helped reduce the amount of pilfering that went on in the stores. In addition to my work schedule, I policed the fitting rooms and helped reduce the amount of stealing. For instance, some women would go into the fitting rooms and exchange their worn and dirty underwear with new ones they had purloined from the sales racks. It was so disgusting to see the untidy used underwear of those otherwise well-dressed women.

Bedford and I kept discussing our situation. We concluded that the best thing we could do for ourselves was to use the opportunity we had, that is our presence in America, to advance ourselves academically. We also had the threat of forced repatriation to Nigeria hanging over our heads. We learned that the Nigerian consulate was persuading the American authorities that we constituted security risks and that former Biafran embassy personnel should all be repatriated to Nigeria. Eventually, we overcame that hurdle. I can't forget how we did that. We had contacted the Nigerian consulate about giving us fresh papers because our Nigerian passports had expired and our Biafran travel documents were of no value. There was reluctance at first, but eventually we were invited to the consulate for interview. I went first.

While I was seated, waiting for my turn, one consulate staff member, a Hausa-speaking fellow began to rain abuses in Hausa language on me and all Biafrans, calling us renegades, bastards, and unbelievers, with the words *Kafiri, Nyamiri* and *Arna* repeatedly in use. Since I speak Hausa, I understood all he was saying. It got to a point where I could not take the abuse any longer, and it didn't matter anymore whether I got the passport or not. I called him and abused him as best as my Hausa would allow, with more invectives in English when my Hausa seemed inadequate.

Meanwhile, as he was abusing me, his boss, rebuked him and said to him in Hausa that he was causing trouble and that his action was in bad taste and unacceptable. I promptly complimented the boss for his mature reaction. The offending staff member was made to apologize to me. I was then called into an inner office, and my passport that should have taken a few days or even weeks to prepare, was given to me on the same day. I was also offered a drink. I wondered whether the outcome was due to the power of language; my ability to speak the Hausa language. The boss asked me if I was born in Kano. He was close to the truth. I was not born in Kano, but I lived there as a young man and, apparently, the Hausa I spoke had clear indications of the language peculiar to the Kano area of northern Nigeria. I had not known that. Subsequently, other former Biafrans who were having difficulty obtaining their papers, were attended to easily if I called up the consulate. I became somewhat of an unofficial consul for Biafrans in need of proper documentation. I was also frequently invited to social activities of the consulate.

After a while, Bedford and I agreed that in order to obtain some free study credits, the best thing to do was to seek employment in a university, even if we'd get less pay than we would get elsewhere. Working in a university automatically allowed one to take some school credits free. Columbia University and the New School for Social Research, both in New York, were the most attractive options. We sought employment at Columbia University. Bedford and I did the reverse of what I did at Alexander's. We agreed that if I flaunted my first-class honors degree, I might not be given the lowly jobs that were the only ones available. I said at the interview that I had only a secondary-school certificate. I was employed as a coffee brewer/server. I also took care of interoffice mail and message delivery.

A series of interesting incidents changed my engagement in Columbia University. My boss was very strict, but he was kindhearted. One day, the departmental secretary was sick. The boss was in distress about some material that needed to be typed. No other person in the office could type. I volunteered to do the typing even though I worried that he would wonder why I was making coffee if I had good typing skills. One of the benefits I earned from my clerical service days was my ability to type. My typing speed was well over forty-five words per minute. My boss was surprised at my request but gave me the manuscripts. I produced the typed material, and he was extremely pleased.

Then he asked the question I had worried about: "Why did you not take a typing job in the first place?"

"A typing position was not advertised." I replied.

Another day, Dr. Obinani Okoli, one of our friends from the Biafran embassy, came to look for me, but I was not around. He got into conversation with my boss and said he was looking for Ambassador Felix Uzoka. (I was no ambassador, but that's what most Biafrans called the embassy personnel.) They then discussed the Biafran struggle and me. When I returned the next day, my boss said to me, "Come here, Felix. Sit down. Who are you?"

My fears were now real. He had found me out. He continued, "You have not told me who you are. Were you really an ambassador?" He told me about the conversation he'd had with Dr. Okoli, and I said to myself, "Obinani has killed me!" I thought I was about to lose my job on account of the lie I told about my qualifications. When I gave him the facts, he laughed and said he was truly impressed with the humility with which I took on the job of a coffee brewer, serving the whole office with much friendliness. He made a point of calling the whole office staff and telling them about me. After this, the joke around the office when I served coffee was, "This is ambassadorial coffee."

The offshoot of this event was that two weeks later, my boss called me and told me that there was a position for a purchasing officer in the physics department. He said he thought I was qualified for the job and advised me to apply. I did, and with his recommendation, I was appointed to the position, which allowed me to take full advantage of the free-credit study at Columbia University and also increased my take-home pay. I immediately registered for the master's degree program in clinical psychology.

Even though I registered for the clinical specialty, I was studying not to become a university professor but only to qualify some more for administrative work, which I so much desired. However, as I progressed with the lectures, I became more and more drawn to the field I had chosen. I sought a full scholarship at Columbia but it was not feasible. I then contacted my erstwhile professor at the University of Nigeria, Professor Edith Lord, who was then at the University of Miami. She was enthusiastic about having me come over. I also applied to other universities. The University of California at Los Angeles offered me a place, but the stipend was too small.

In the meantime, the University of Miami decided to consider me a veteran and awarded me a Veteran Administration (VA) scholarship. The VA scholarship offered very substantial funding. I had not applied for it, knowing that I was not a veteran of any American war. I did not know why they made that offer; indeed, I did not even fully understand the offer, but I accepted it. One month after I arrived in Miami, they found out it was an error and withdrew the scholarship. I was then obliged to depend on one or the other of departmentally funded support and had to do a number of odd jobs (including work as a nurse's aide) to keep myself in the program. Susan and four of the children had joined me then and I needed additional income to take care of the family

Entering the University in Miami and coming under the influence of Professor Edith Lord again, as well as a number of other distinguished clinicians and top scholars, my interest in an academic and clinical life was kindled. I began gradually to change my life goal from permanent secretary to clinician\academic. I immersed myself in the clinical field, and that has been my life. Graduate school was pleasant but riddled with anxiety. Several students who were ahead of my class, had not yet graduated and peddled around the funny title of ABD (All But Dissertation). That is, they had finished all course work but had their dissertation pending, sometimes for more than seven or eight years!

The doctoral program was challenging. My class consisted initially of fourteen people. After the master's degree, there were only five of us left. The rest had been weeded out. You could be dismissed for any of several reasons: substandard class work, clinical incompetence, and so on. Then there was the pre-doctoral qualification examination, the Doctoral Comprehensive Examination and an alternative, the Major Area Paper. Many people failed at this point. Candidates had only two chances to pass the examination; if they failed, they were eased out of the program. There often was no question of going to the university senate for long debates about people to be dismissed. People went away once they were told they were no longer fit to be in the program. I was the only black student, the first ever for postgraduate work in clinical psychology since the inception of the department. I told Susan that we should keep our luggage packed, so that we could return to Nigeria if I failed. Fortunately, I did pretty well, passing the comprehensive examination at the first sitting, along with only one of my classmates, Ross McCrimmon. The others had to try a second and final time. I also completed and defended my doctoral thesis successfully, being the first one in my class to do so.

Very soon, I began to tutor younger students and I began to like teaching. I also enjoyed my clinical assignments. I had several clinical placements, at the Mailman Center for Child Development and the Florida State (Psychiatric) Hospital, among others. I was employed as a psychologist at the Dade County Department of Youth and Family Services. Upon completion of my doctorate, I was employed as assistant professor at the university, teaching undergraduate courses and seminars to postgraduate students. I finally accepted that I had found my niche. Clinical work, especially, gave me so much joy. It felt good to help people pull themselves out of debilitating depression, anxiety, or even graver pathology. My dream of an administrative career was dead.

The Coral Gables campus of the University of Miami was and still is a beautiful campus. There is a stream that runs through the campus with freshwater fish that can be caught with hooks. We lived in front of the stream and fished there often. The university environment was exotic, with a wide variety of trees and plants. The campus was like some gigantic picturesque garden. The entire city of Miami was full of entertainment for both the young and old. The social environment was multicultural, and so we were very well received on campus and in Miami generally. The children enjoyed their stay there. We left Miami in December 1977 and returned to Nigeria.

In 1999, Susan and I went on an emotionally satisfying trip to Miami. I had been invited by the University of Miami to receive the university's Alumnus of the Year Award for outstanding contributions to my field. Susan and I took the opportunity to renew our acquaintance with the environment and with our many friends who were still there. Our daughter, Adaeze Susan, who was staying with her family in Atlanta, accompanied us on the trip. It was a wonderful trip. My former clinical supervisor, Professor Richard Carrera, with his beautiful wife, took us to our favorite Miami beachfront and hosted us at a noonday lunch in a restaurant with many boats moored close by and water birds flying about. We also saw another of my distinguished professors, Ed Murray, and his wife, a professor of nursing. They entertained us and Mrs. Murray told me that she found one of my scientific papers on family dynamics an excellent material for her teaching. That was heartwarming. She was visibly excited when I told her that Columbia University had requested my permission to publish the material in their tutorial text. We took time to see the former head of the department, Bob Jones. Professor Jones, a distinguished scholar, had established his reputation on studies of motivation. We met him and his wife at their condo, and it was obvious that his health was failing. But he was, as always, in excellent spirits, with unceasing good humor. We talked about old times; he, a seasoned aviator, who once flew his plane as a hobby around the country, was now practically homebound. It was the other side of aging, beyond the joys of leisure in retirement. He and his wife were overjoyed to see us. Two days after we left Miami for Atlanta, we got the sad news that he had passed away in his sleep.

Susan and I explored parts of the campus of the university on foot, taking in old haunts, and admiring new structures and the breathtaking environment. We had breakfast in the old but revamped students' center. As we walked about, I recalled that my doctoral academic gown—which I often use for ceremonial occasions in Nigeria, such as matriculations and convocations—was faded and torn. I walked into the Students' Affairs Office and requested for a new one, offering to pay for it. The gown, cap, and tassels were issued to me at once, free of charge. The department and the school's dean feted Susan and me. At the award ceremony on May 24, 1999, I delivered a presentation titled "Psychology in Nigeria and Psychology's Global Agenda for the New Millennium." The presentation was well received, and the excerpts published in the University of Miami's journal.

Chapter 17

University Service in Nigeria: The Very Good, the Bad, and the Truly Ugly

We returned to Nigeria in 1977, and I became a lecturer at the University of Nigeria, Nsukka. It was a good homecoming. We were delighted to be back home. Although I had been appointed to the University of Nigeria, I was still legally a staff member of the Ministry of Agriculture. I went and sought transfer from the Ministry to the university, since they were both government establishments. We had initial accommodation problems, but I soon settled down into the academic routine. The late 1970s was a good time in the universities and in the country generally. The national currency, the naira, was healthy and sought after. The era of decay was yet to come. Teachers were serious with their work, and students were eager to learn. A distinguished scholar, Professor Tam David-West, has described the 1960s and '70s as the "era of bloom" in Nigerian universities, when scholarship was at its apex, that is, until the era of gloom in the mid-1980s. I was also privileged to hold active positions in a number of professional bodies and this involved extensive travel within and outside Nigeria. I certainly had my share of trips to Europe; East, West and Southern Africa; Canada; and the United States.

I enjoyed my teaching assignments and also my clinical practice. Faculty would give lectures as late as from 8 p.m. to 10 p.m. It was a truly academic atmosphere. Conferences organized by academic and professional bodies were serious matters and were held regularly. In fact, as head of department, I queried staff who failed to attend conferences. Publishing research work was celebrated. If someone published a research paper, especially in a reputable foreign journal, that event was celebrated and launched with drinks; "washed" was the term applied to the event. In Nigeria, intense scholarly exchange between scholars was the order of the day. Work was truly pleasurable and rewarding. There was considerable camaraderie among the lecturers, and students worked hard. Sorting (negotiating for grades) and other vices that eroded the educational system had not yet become common practice.

There were deficiencies, but the spirit of the institution, faculty, scholars, and students was clearly focused on doing everything possible to promote academic goals and intellectual endeavors. In the beginning, I had no clinical facilities to speak of, and I had to build from scratch. What facilitated my work was that I took on cases within the community in collaboration with the university medical center, charging only token fees. For example, patients that ordinarily would have gone to the Psychiatric Centre in Enugu, with significant expenses, would be required to pay only a token fee of ten kobo (less than ten cents) for consultations, assessment, and psychotherapy at our clinic. After numerous successful interventions, I soon popularized the field within the university.

I mentioned to the faculty officer, Churchill Adimora, that I was looking for space to set up the Psychological Services Centre; at that time, accommodation was tight. He was eager to help me. I had successfully managed in therapy his failing relative who was then finishing his studies. He went around to the various facilities and immediately identified an excellent classroom, which had an adjoining toilet. I converted it into the Psychological Services Centre, where the facility is still located today. I was able to introduce essential training items, such as audiovisuals and a one-way mirror for unobtrusive observation and supervision.

Funding the clinic facility remained a problem, but this was solved in another interesting way. I was in Lagos for a conference, and I was ready to get back to Nsukka. I went to the university liaison office to see if I could hitch a ride with any officials who came to Lagos. I was in luck. The university bursar, Mr. Chris Ezike, was planning to travel on the same day and gladly offered me a ride. On our way, I mentioned the center's financial problems to him. He asked, "Isn't that where you treat the people referred to you, where you treated my niece?" I said that it was, and he recalled how much I had helped his niece. He said, "Why don't you make a case for the Centre to get its own budget as a regular expenditure item of the university?"

I did so, and with his support, the Psychological Services Centre was included in the university budget and had its own funding. This truly enhanced our teaching at both the undergraduate and postgraduate levels and facilitated our participation in professional conferences.

So, while I did not make any personal gains from my clinical services,

I certainly advanced the position of the discipline through the services I rendered within and beyond the university community. It did not stop there. We had a need for biofeedback instrumentation used in measuring various physiological reactions associated with emotional states. I went to the vice chancellor, Professor Frank Ndili, and made a case for the equipment. He told me to refine the documentation of my request and the price came to about $26,000, a substantial sum. At that time, the universities operated accounts in foreign banks. The funds were released promptly, the order placed, and within two months the equipment arrived from the United States. Our center became equipped at a level comparable to those overseas. A foreign external examiner was surprised at the extent and quality of the facilities we had.

The mention of Professor Ndili reminds me of the nature, stature, and styles of the vice chancellors (or university presidents) I have come across and worked with during my years in the university system. As a psychologist, I observed the varying personalities of these university administrators. One common characteristic was their outsized egos. Perhaps, it had to be so. To lead a group of colleagues in an arena where intelligence and scholarship constituted the yardstick of measurement, one had to be especially convinced about one's intellectual capabilities. It is clear, of course, based on several cases of inefficiency in university governance, that quite a few of those leaders were misguided about their capabilities and therefore overrated themselves. The situation in the universities often did not provide opportunities for broad leadership training. There were major differences in style as well as orientation. Three vice chancellors stand out in my estimation for their good leadership, clarity of goals, and commitment to institutional development. They also, in my professional assessment, had well-integrated personalities, without unduly disabling neurotic tendencies. They are Professor Frank Ndili, a distinguished physicist, whose contributions to the development of the University of Nigeria, Nsukka, remain unequalled. Professor Nurudeen Alao of the University of Lagos was a good administrator who kept his eyes well focused on the need for institutional growth. Professor Festus Nwako of Nnamdi Azikiwe University, Awka, was a renowned pediatric surgeon, whose leadership style created an atmosphere that supported intellectual endeavor and made him a legend within the institution and perhaps beyond. (Fittingly, the ultra-modern university library was subsequently named the Festus Aghagbo Nwako Library.)

Like all humans, these leaders were not without fault, but they had one major attribute going for them. They were sound scholars, and they kept the goal of intellectual advancement of their institutions clear and focused. They administered their various institutions without the ethnic or sectional orientation that soon would overtake many Nigerian universities. One afternoon, when I was dean of the School of Postgraduate Studies, I was summoned to Professor Nwako's office, because of a report that the school had failed to offer admission to a young man who bore his surname. The prospective student turned out to be Professor Nwako's nephew. He had applied for admission, but his application was late. However, the matter was improperly presented to the vice chancellor. Professor Nwako had received calls regarding the young man and asked me what happened. I gave him the necessary documentation. He said to me, "Do *not* offer him admission!" with great emphasis on the word "not."

In my presence, he admonished the young man for not taking his future seriously and said directly to him, "In this institution, we operate on regulations and deadlines. You should apply on time, next time around if you are truly serious about postgraduate studies. I have always told you to take your future seriously."

That was truly impressive. Professor Festus Nwako had another rare characteristic among institutional leaders. He hated gossip. One university engineer had a sad tale to tell. He had heard that someone was maligning the vice chancellor but did not investigate the matter properly before rushing to Professor Nwako to narrate the story. Professor Nwako asked him to sit in the adjoining waiting room and, without his knowledge, promptly sent for the party mentioned. When the engineer was called back into the vice chancellor's office, he found the fellow he had been gossiping about seated there. Professor Nwako asked him to narrate his story again. He was hugely embarrassed. The situation was especially bad for him because there was no truth to the narrative he presented to the vice chancellor. He said he learned not to gossip ever again. Professor Nwako ran an open and transparent administration, the kind that is rarely found anymore. Institutional administration has since become a cabal, with the real goals of institutions rarely considered. Institutional goals are now subordinated to ethnic and sectional interests with the cabal's survival as the overriding focus

Within the university system, I had stints as head of department during the years 1982–86, and 1990–91. I also served as consultant clinical psychologist with the university medical center and at several other schools. At Nnamdi Azikiwe University, I served as head of department briefly in 1991, and then as dean of the Faculty of Social Sciences for two terms (1992–93 and 2002–2004). I was dean of the School of Postgraduate Studies from 1994 to 1999 and director of consultancy services in 1999. I was a member of the Governing Council of Nnamdi Azikiwe University from 1997 to 1999. I had earlier also engaged in trade union activity and was elected branch chairman of the Academic Staff Union of Universities (ASUU) at the University of Nigeria. In 1986, I was promoted to the rank of professor at the University of Nigeria, Nsukka, and in 1987, I became a professor at the University of Lagos for a period of two years. I returned to the University of Nigeria in 1989 to complete my thirty-five-year service before taking an early retirement in 1991 at the age of fifty-six, just when I felt I was truly maturing as an academic. At that time, retirement for academic staff was mandatory for people who had rendered thirty-five years of continuous service in the public service or had reached the age of sixty years. Subsequently, I took up a contract appointment with Nnamdi Azikiwe University, until I was seventy and no longer qualified, according to the law, to continue in the public service.

My service with the ASUU was during the heyday of university trade unionism, and it was wonderful to see the enthusiasm and patriotism of union leaders. As chairman of the union branch at my university, I worked closely with the then national president, Dr. Mahmud Tukur, who was teaching at Ahmadu Bello University in Zaria. Dr. Tukur's lifestyle and philosophy were admirable. He was simple in his way of life, and his concerns were always for other people. He was deeply concerned about the development of education in the country and with enhancing the morale of teachers to promote greater commitment.

We held one meeting in the town of Maiduguri in the far north of the country. The sessions were long and tedious. In exhaustion and because he had a troubling health condition, Dr. Tukur would simply lie down on the bare floor, take a brief nap, and then wake up for another round of long, exhausting meetings. He never allowed his own discomfort to interfere with the work of the union. He was also a real academic and an avid historian. Once, on a trip to my own base at the University of Nigeria, Nsukka, for a meeting of the National Executive Committee (NEC), he insisted that I take him to Enugu to see the Nigerian nationalist and author Mokwugo Okoye from whom he wanted to buy some books. His schedule was a tight one, and we left Nsukka at about 8 p.m. and got to Mokwugo Okoye's Enugu residence at about 9 p.m. Mahmud wanted all of Mukwugo's available books, *African Responses*, *The Beard of Prometheus*, and others. He placed an order for those that were not available in Nigeria. It was pleasant to see such a scholar of note appreciating the work of a fellow Nigerian. By the time we got back to Nsukka, it was past midnight.

Although I was working in Nsukka, only seventy kilometers from Enugu, I had not read Mokwugo's writings until Mahmud introduced them to me. I did not understand his fascination with Mokwugo until I bought the books and read them myself. I have not stopped reading them. A lover of history myself, it was *African Responses* that opened my eyes to a fresh, radical interpretation of African history and a deeper appreciation of African contributions to world civilization. My earlier love for history was rekindled. I wonder even today how Mokwugo Okoye, a man, initially with only a secondary-school education, produced such classics. Mokwugo Okoye's books were required reading for all Mahmud Tukur's students, particularly his postgraduate students. Mahmud Tukur's death was a real loss to the ASUU and scholarship in Nigeria.

University politics was one massive experience. I saw the good, the bad, and the truly ugly in human nature in the encounters I witnessed. People were motivated by a mixture of personal greed and the desire for power and position, a scenario that one would not normally associate with the pristine academic setting expected in a university. Because I was chairman of the union in my university, people would come to me with grandiose ideas about institutional change based on what they insisted were basic inviolable principles of justice, fair play, and equity. However, as soon as they realized that their personal (sometimes mundane and pedestrian) interests would not be satisfied, they would disappear and so would their avowed "inviolable" principles that they earlier ardently professed and promoted! Gradually, religion and ethnicity came to aid personal interests, and the university system became truly polarized not because of intellectual and academic matters, as one would wish, but because of personal interests and greed.

The change of guard in the university, that is the change in leadership (the office of vice chancellor/president), was especially a season for murderous conflicts, sometimes degenerating into physical violence and, in some cases, recourse to juju and medicine men. Religious differences within Christianity or between Christianity and Islam were exploited to the fullest. Ideology and principles became alien notions in the university due to these conflicts. Intra-tribal animosities and rivalries were also at play. The tragedy of all of this was that scholarship suffered due to the lingering effects of the divisions that emerged. Discussions would center on who was supporting the incumbent vice chancellor, if he or she was up for possible reappointment, or the other candidates.

Quite perceptibly, the overall climate of the universities changed. Some of the indicators of change were troubling. The atmosphere of scholarly debates was practically lost. Many scholars generally neglected their calling, and attendance at professional conferences also diminished. Journal publication became a rarity. More troubling was the fact that our very good students, the outstanding first-class honors group and the second-class upper division group, were unwilling to take up academic careers. Instead, they went for lucrative bank jobs and even to the police force. That was good for these establishments, but it was a terribly bad omen for the academic growth and renewal of the universities and the country. The students had good reasons not to join the teaching profession. Lecturers had become lowly teachers, poorly paid; for many, the motivation to teach was gone. In the climate of military rule which began in 1966 and lasted for over two decades, intellectual matters were neglected or even directly stymied. Education was not considered a serious national issue. Power was the issue, and clearly the military men did not need education to carry their guns for their coups! Facilities deteriorated. Institutions derailed.

Then the snowball effects emerged. First was the menace of handouts. Teachers, unwilling to engage in effective teaching, resorted to handouts. These usually consisted of old materials purloined or plagiarized from books, typed, and sold to students as a means of making additional income. Sorting (buying) of grades also emerged (i.e., paying for grades in one form or the other). Students offered gratification to teachers to obtain desired grades, or teachers demanded gratification to grant unearned grades. Teachers were not teaching well, and students had no desire to apply themselves. The situation suited both the teachers and the students.

This situation had grave effects on teaching and learning. The relationship between teachers and students became blurred. The tradition of the teacher enjoying the act of imparting knowledge to his or her students and often also learning from students' creative endeavors, increasingly diminished. One of the thrills of teaching is to be challenged by young minds with new ideas or old ideas recast in refreshingly new light. Particularly at the level of postgraduate teaching, a good teacher encourages students to think independently, to ask questions, and to express ideas freely no matter how outrageous they may seem. Such teachers reap bountiful dividends in the growing creativity of students, as well as, acquire new learning for themselves. When I became active in postgraduate supervision, I was able to fully appreciate the routine statement of one of my major supervisors when I was in school myself. Professor Richard Carrera would say to us that any student for the masters or doctoral degree from whom he had not learned something, had not done any useful work. In Nigeria, all this was largely lost because of the diminishing interest in matters of intellect. Even to get students to agree to work on teachers' projects as a learning base for their own research efforts, as was the case elsewhere, was increasingly rejected by the new breed of students. The routine statement one heard was, "I am not going to be used by him or her [the teacher] to do research to get his or her promotion." So, how did the student expect to learn?

The joys of the teacher were largely abandoned. Once in the 1980s, my erstwhile teacher and head of department in the 1960s, John Anowi came to visit. I was then the head of department. When he walked into my office, I stood up to greet him, and I was clearly uncomfortable sitting down again in the chair that he had once occupied. I kept standing. He saw my discomfort, laughed, pointed to the chair, and asked me (I felt he ordered me) to sit down.

He said, "You are trying to deny me the joys of a teacher. You sitting down there is my joy that one of my bright students has risen to be in that chair. I am proud of you."

I felt both proud and humbled by his approval. Making a positive difference in young lives was the teacher's ultimate reward. Clearly, for my former teacher, grooming the next generation and enjoying their development and prosperity was his prime gratification.

Negotiations for grades in return for various considerations, including money, sex, and other things, were painful for many of us, especially the old guard lecturers for whom grades were sacrosanct and for whom the obligation to teach, to impart knowledge, was the very life of the teacher. As was to be expected, a few pathetic old guard fellows, propelled by poverty and greed, also joined in the erosion of academic culture. Teachers were not alone in this malaise. Students liked the changed circumstances of not really working for their grades. Young female students unabashedly propositioned teachers, even those who were old enough to be their fathers or even older, in the bid to obtain unearned grades.

The changed circumstances in the university got me into a lot of conflict with the newer breed of teachers, themselves products of an eroded educational system. My protestations and those of my like-minded colleagues brought abuses on us. We were tagged as "ancient men" who do not know "what is on" or "where it's at." (The Igbo phrase "ebe ano" [where it's at] was most popular.) We were ridiculed as those who believe that teachers should die poor. One particular lecturer was a former student of mine; at the height of his misbehaviors, and with no formal administrative injunctions by the authorities restraining him, I sought to call him to order. I reminded him that when I taught him at the master's level, I bought drinks and snacks for everyone during my lectures. Where then, I asked, did he learn that the reverse—taking money and gifts from students, often by force—was appropriate behavior? He looked at me with a rather pitying stare, mumbled something inaudible, and shrugged off my question! I guess he still had some respect for my age, if not for my status as his former teacher and very senior colleague, and so avoided insulting me directly. Where did I, did we, go wrong, I thought to myself.

Things went beyond just being ridiculed. Some of my own postgraduate students refused to undertake basic class assignments. One particular case was truly painful for me. One of the young lecturers in my department had registered for doctoral work after completing a master's program with me. I was instrumental to his being appointed as a graduate assistant, earlier on. I gave him five books in specialized areas in the field to read, including one very important book I had just acquired from a recent trip to the United States. He read only two, threw the whole pack into my mailbox, and brazenly stated in an open departmental meeting, "I have read enough," and proceeded to create political steam by insisting that I was wasting his time. In two years of part-time study for a doctoral degree, however, he had done no work. Academic work with him soon became the fire for inter-town (intra tribal) bickering, with some academic administrators siding with the young man. The idea for these misguided pseudo-intellectuals was that time spent on the program and what the young man was willing to do, were enough to grant him a Ph.D. I refused to succumb to such intimidation.

In the heat of the politicized academics, the young man was brazen enough to write a copious petition against me to the establishment, listing against me the ills I had been advising him to avoid. Rev. Canon Israel Okoye, a decent gentleman and a distinguished scholar who succeeded me as dean of Faculty, asked him whether what he wrote was true. He said no but added that because there was a quarrel, he was free to invent anything he wanted. Elements from within the establishment, motivated by sectional and clan interests, encouraged his offensiveness. This was while he was facing a panel of inquiry for sexual harassment of a female student and subsequently was twice caught selling university entry admission, a felonious and chargeable offence. Sometime later, much later, in a new wave of institutional renewal, he was suspended following confirmed reports of his admission racketeering and his townspeople, including the traditional ruler (*igwe*), went to his aid in fighting the institution's decision.

Clearly, the academe had begun to reflect the larger society in which corruption, greed, selfish pursuits, tribal and ethnic leanings, and the routine acceptance of mediocrity pervaded the social system. The town, like an invasive virus, had infected and overwhelmed the gown. The contrast with earlier days was painfully sharp. In 1984, a doctoral thesis I supervised, with an expatriate scholar serving as external examiner, was so well done that the student and I won the award for scholarly excellence at the University of Nigeria. The external examiner was very impressed with the standard of scholarship in the thesis. That is not the case anymore!

Not too long ago, one of the younger professors told his young colleagues that it was a sin to come to work with an empty pocket and go home with an empty pocket. One wonders what wares he brought to the university to sell. Many lecturers became quite brazen in their exploitation of the students. One of them, whose professorship was in question, had the effrontery to prepare a list of students who had to pay him two thousand naira apiece (the equivalent of about $15), to pass his course, which they had purportedly failed. The list was in his own handwriting. That's how brazen, and perhaps stupid, he had become. At that time, he had not yet released the full official class results as required by the university academic regulations, and his department had not reviewed the results in line with the practice in the university. Thankfully, the university administration, in a new wave of cleansing, suspended and then sacked the erring professor. There might yet be sanity again. He has gone to court to seek redress, to seek equity and fairness, rights that he did not accord his young wards.

It is proper to mention, however, that in all this chaos, there were oases that kept hope alive. There was still a core of dedicated teachers, and many students who desired to learn, enjoyed learning, and made teaching a worthwhile and rewarding enterprise. I remember some of my outstanding doctoral students as Bernice Ezeilo, now Professor Ezeilo, Dr. Mike Ezenwa, Dr. Harry Obi-Nwosu, Dr. (Rev.) Nkwam Uwaoma, and many other postgraduate students who were committed to sound and rigorous scholarship and distinguished themselves. From them, I derive some hope that scholarship will still thrive in our environment.

Of course the real change will come when federal, state, and local governments pay proper attention to education and recognize that no developmental effort will succeed or be sustainable, unless education receives priority attention. That is the orientation in the developed world. Sound education and enlightenment are the basis of their continuing progress and supremacy. The failings of the university system and, indeed, the entire educational enterprise in Nigeria, represent the failure of governance, the failure of leadership to be preoccupied with the future of the nation and with posterity. It reflects the absence of visionary leadership. Years of neglect by succeeding military governments totally eroded the earlier outstanding intellectual culture of Nigeria. In addition, Nigerian history—so replete with routine looting of the national treasury by the leadership (military and civilian)—represents the misplacement of personal and national values and the lack of accountability. Only a fresh orientation in leadership will refocus national attention on the imperative of sound education and promote sustainable national development. Such reorientation will foster proper investment in education, funding and refurbishment of institutions, adequate remuneration for teachers, unalloyed and sustained support for research, rejection of mediocrity, and a healthy attitude to matters of intellect, with adequate national acclaim for scholarly achievements.

Chapter 18

The Joys of Clinical Work

One of the most satisfying life conditions is the practice of clinical psychology. Helping people regain their mental equilibrium and bringing peace to troubled minds and troubled relationships has been a source of great joy for me, perhaps to the extent of neglecting the possible financial gains. The joyful faces of clients and their families and friends at the end of successful therapy, are truly gratifying. As I rummage through hundreds of my work records, I recall that so many of the cases were rewarding experiences. (Names and initials of clients and some demographics have been altered to ensure anonymity.)

Mrs. A

Mrs. A came to our clinic at the Psychological Services Centre, Nsukka, from Britain. She had gone to Britain several times for the treatment of a condition. On the last trip, they diagnosed her condition as psychological/ psychosomatic, and she was told to see a clinical psychologist. The physician in Britain was aware of my practice and referred her to me. This patient was the wife of a well-known national figure, a politician of note. Her case was challenging. She had distress enough to cause considerable concern. She was in psychotherapy with me for a period of six months and regained full functional health.

One interesting feature of this case was that I required the husband to attend most of the treatment sessions since, based on my assessment, there were some negative transactional family features in the case, that is, that interpersonal relationships in the family were faulty. The husband readily agreed. Often in clinical practice in Nigeria, many spouses, usually the men, are unwilling to participate in psychotherapy. This is because they often perceive the process as acknowledging that there is emotional distress in their family and that they have failed to "manage" their family effectively. The denial that an emotional illness is present is still strong within the society. This particular husband, however, was enlightened and most cooperative, often flying in from some distance away just to attend a two-hour session.

At the termination of a very successful therapeutic process, they asked about my fee. I told them that the treatment was given in courtesy to the family (a rather unprofessional response, right?). They went away, but subsequent events showed that they were not pleased. Three years later, I received a certified check for a very substantial sum, via a colleague at the university, with a note pleading with me not to reject the money. They seemed so anxious to express their appreciation for my intervention and perhaps were troubled that they had not done so, even after such a long time. I had saved them not only from the stress associated with ill-health but also from the substantial expense of going abroad for treatment. Despite the prevailing stigma regarding mental-health matters, this couple never ceases to tell people how I helped the wife regain her health. My wife and I are invited to their significant family events. I cashed the check.

This case reminded me of my reluctance to receive gifts in general, which has affected my attitude to fees for clinical work. My professional colleagues have chided me for not empowering the field with regard to fees, that is, to promote the awareness that fees for psychological services rendered is proper. At Eastern Pennsylvania Psychiatric Institute in Philadelphia, where I did my pre-doctoral clinical internship, I had a client with a psychiatric condition. Through my therapy intervention, he regained his health and began to perform very well in school. His parents celebrated their son's recovery with a vacation in Egypt and brought me gifts from their trip. I showed some hesitancy in accepting the gifts, and one of my supervisors, Dr. Betty Ignatowski, yelled at me over the intercom phone. (She was behind a one-way mirror, unobtrusively observing the therapy session.) She said, "Felix, can't you accept gifts graciously?" I then beamed a smile at the family and thanked them profusely for the gifts: a room-thermometer, a beautiful necktie, and a gong made of clay, with Egyptian engravings on the sides. I still have the necktie, thirty-one years later, and I am amazed at how long ties can last, becoming fashionable in alternating periods of fashion.

After the patient and his family left, Dr. Ignatowski (a great clinician) said I should examine myself and recognize why I had difficulty in receiving. How else, she asked, could patients express their gratitude for the work I had done for them, beyond the official fees? Dr. Ignatowski classified me as having a character complex that enjoys giving but avoids receiving. According to her, accepting a gift puts the receiver in debt to the other person, and so some people seek to avoid that sense of indebtedness. She reasoned that a receiver feels psychologically beholden to the giver, but a generous giver should be willing to allow others to experience the joy of giving. That, she said, is an essential element of reciprocity in human relationships. More significantly, a gift voluntarily presented to the therapist at the end of treatment is a useful gauge of the success of the therapy and of patient satisfaction. True, there was something to her ideas. Even though at the time I was not totally in agreement with her analysis, I certainly had and still have difficulty with accepting gifts outside of my family. One dilemma for me, particularly in the context of broader social encounters, remains the thin boundary between receiving in appreciative gratitude, and bribery.

Miss J

Miss J was a longtime patient at the psychiatric hospital. She was diagnosed with manic depression, now referred to as bipolar illness. She was sometimes in a wild state and got very little sleep; at other times, she would be intensely depressed and physically immobile. She was also suicidal. She was a grossly overweight individual who had very low self-esteem. She was unemployed at the time and depended on welfare payments. She was placed on lithium and other drugs. She was assigned to me for psychotherapy. One night, at 1 a.m., a phone call woke me up. It was hospital personnel, who said that Miss J had had a very bad episode and was threatening to jump off the ledge of a top-floor window. She was asking for me. They wanted me to come and talk her out of committing suicide. She had refused to talk to anyone else but me.

I arrived at the hospital and began a difficult, four-hour, interaction with my client. She said, "Look at me, my life, and tell me one reason why I should live."

I said, "Come on, Miss J. Let's talk about that, let's figure that out. We always do, don't we? I am here so we can figure things out. I am here for you, Miss J."

It was quite a harrowing experience to feel that a life depended on my intervention. I don't recall another situation in my practice in which my heart was racing to that extent as I sought to help a patient. In the end, as twilight arrived, I was able to engage her not only with language but also with eye contact. In time, she made a crucial movement and extended her hand to me and I gently tugged her away from danger. I felt great relief and spent the rest of the morning in the hospital with her, taking no breakfast and leaving only when she fell asleep. Over a period of six months, she stayed on a stable course and was placed in a rehabilitation facility, where she found some meaning in life. I continued to see her in psychotherapy with diminishing regularity until I left the facility. It was rewarding for me to see her make some progress.

Master M. C.

Master M. C. was a medical student, well into the fifth year of study. He was reportedly a very good student but became disoriented and could not continue his studies. His parents were both medical personnel; the father was a longtime medical specialist, and the mother was a high-ranking nurse. The parents took the young man to various hospitals and specialist centers with little success. At one university-based institution, a lobotomy was suggested. The parents also sought the help of traditional healers and faith healers. Somewhere along in their search, they were referred to our clinic.

The young man was truly disturbed, with deep depression, diminished alertness, and significantly slow physical functions. He also had both visual and auditory hallucinations. He protested that he did not want to continue with his medical studies and wanted to get into cabinet-making. He was one of three children and had two sisters. The parents said they would be quite happy if he was well and that his career choice was irrelevant. Cabinet making was okay by them. I stopped the numerous medications he was on, particularly the more recent pharmaceutical products. In my practice, I have found some of the newer medicines, particularly antidepressants, to cause more problems for some patients, particularly because of their often uncertain side effects, not to mention the high costs. But the drug companies continue to promote them with aggressive advertising that targets especially doctors. Some of our medical personnel, especially non-psychiatrists operating in psychiatric centers, also do not quickly respond to the research findings on drug effects. I find the older drugs to be more dependable, with more manageable side effects and more predictable patient responses. The parents agreed with my treatment regimen.

After three months of psychotherapy, the young man was able to return to school; he performed very well and came within the first ten positions in the final results. He received an automatic internship at his school, passed his screening, and became a full-fledged medical doctor. He got married right away and went overseas. In a year, his parents became grandparents, after the birth of his daughter. He passed his medical certification exams in America and now is placed in a specialist course. Susan and I are always invited as valued guests to the family's activities and the father tells anyone within earshot how I saved his only son's life and career. To protect the young man's interests, I am the one who restrains the father from talking so freely about his son's ailment because of the prevailing social stigma. It gladdens the heart to think about the healing of this wonderful, brilliant young man and many others who have gone through successful therapy with us.

Master R. A.

Another case that gave me great joy was that of R. A. He was a young man of nineteen who had become homebound, and was placed on a variety of medicines at the nearby psychiatric center. He experienced no relief. The father, an archdeacon, and his wife were distraught and did not know what to do with this young man who needed to be attended to regularly and chaperoned whenever he left the house. On a number of occasions when he'd gone out alone, he could not find his way home. The young man also underwent psychiatric treatment in Benin. The parents consulted various native doctors and faith healers. But he experienced no relief. By the time he was referred to our facility, he had a comatose look, with his nostrils dripping—no, flowing—with heavy mucous. In any one day, he would use up three or more rolls of toilet tissue. His nose was never dry. His gait was hesitant and sluggish. He actually wobbled along and was held by the hand. He was hardly coherent in his speech. But although he appeared moody, the psychological assessment protocols showed no clear-cut indices of psychopathology beyond retardation in physical activity. The parents had consulted a medical doctor on this, but he offered only palliatives. It was a puzzling case.

I worked with the young man for about three months, and he showed very little improvement. After repeated sessions of psychotherapy, I began to think about other reasons for his condition. In my practice, I routinely focus on the total person and usually seek a full medical review. In this particular instance, the possibility of an allergic condition occurred to me. This had not been addressed by his previous medical treatment. The family eventually agreed that I could begin an exclusion process to identify and remove known possible allergy sources from his diet, although initially, they did not see my point. I imagine that the parents felt they had come to the psychologist to deal with their son's mental-health problems, and here was I dealing with his diet. However, their son's state and the fact that they had explored other options unsuccessfully, must have persuaded them to agree to try my prescription. We began a trial-and-error process to detect particular food items or substances that could cause allergies.

Within two months we found the culprit: crayfish. The patient was extremely allergic to seafood. In fact, he had mentioned earlier on that one of his distastes was crayfish. Here was a case of a personal distaste being unknowingly related to the source of a health condition. When crayfish was removed from his menu, he recovered quickly. He lost his comatose look and fumbling gait. His nose dried up. He joined the university a year later. He graduated in accountancy and is now working overseas. The family has remained appreciative of my intervention. This case points to the fact that various medical personnel do not pay enough attention to allergy conditions— whether due to genetics or prescription medicines—in the management of physical and psychiatric symptoms. I have come across some cases of drug-induced allergy in which the attending medical personnel did not determine the cause of the allergy or even sought to withdraw the offending drug.

Miss A. W.

This patient was referred to me from another psychiatric treatment facility. The family had also consulted several native doctors, but there was no change in the young lady's condition. When she arrived at the clinic, she was disoriented, sluggish, and was drooling quite profusely. Psychological assessment revealed a depressed and crestfallen mood. She was at that point heavily sedated on a variety of psychiatric drugs. She was a third-year accountancy student but had been away from the university for nearly a year because of her condition. The family was greatly conflicted and fractured. The husband and wife were at loggerheads on practically every matter, from feeding to childrearing to sex. The husband was himself on psychiatric medication for depression. The wife carried herself in a state of permanent anguish over both her marriage and the problems of her children. She felt that she had married beneath herself even though her husband was an engineer. She was very unhappy with her station in life. The young girl had been the victim of continuous rape and sexual abuse by her eldest brother, spanning several years. The brother later abandoned the home and left the country, settling in another African country and even marrying there. He had very minimal communication between himself and the family.

With the attending physician, I counseled the minimization of the drug regimen and instituted psychotherapy. As therapy progressed, the conflict within the young lady became clear. For example, although she said that she was a victim of the brother's rape, she also missed him intensely. In a strange twist, she had fallen in love with him, sought every possible opportunity to contact him by phone and letters, and was in pain if she did not hear from him. This says something about the need for clinicians to tread with caution in situations of incest because of the conflicting emotions that are usually involved. The young lady was also conflicted about other unstable love relationships she had experienced. She had difficulty loving anyone but her brother. She was conflicted about her parents' discord. She was conflicted about establishing any permanent relationships with men or women. Overwhelmed, she withdrew and became sick.

After four months of intensive psychotherapy, sometimes meeting twice in one day, as well as marital therapy with the parents, the young lady recovered, returned to school, passed her degree examinations, and participated in the National Youth Service program, the program of a one-year social service that is mandatory for students on completion of university education. She has remained healthy and symptom free for more than six years.

Mrs. S. J.

Mrs. S. J. was a forty-five-year-old woman who was married to a senior faculty member at a university. She was a schoolteacher with a degree in the social sciences. She had been referred to our clinic because of a distressful physical condition diagnosed as psychosomatic by physicians in the United States. She had a variety of disabling physical symptoms that prevented her from attending school or performing house chores. The major problem was severe and excruciating neck pain, accompanied by headaches and visual problems. The neck pain had not responded to medical treatment. She had continued on a drug that had been prescribed for her in California, where she'd studied, and she was about to make another trip to the United States for a reevaluation. Full medical assessment revealed no identifiable physical pathology.

Regular psychological assessment using appropriate protocols, however, revealed the presence of severe depression, anxiety, insomnia, and some suicidal tendencies. Family assessment revealed the presence of considerable conflicts and stress in her life, particularly in her marriage. Although both partners were educated, their relationship within the home was strictly traditional, with the husband exercising absolute and draconian authority over the wife and the children. The wife could not leave the house without permission and without stating clearly where she was going and when she would be back. Sometimes, permission was not granted, even when she wanted to go to the salon! The children were in total awe of their father and disappeared as soon as he came home. The mode of relating between the husband and wife was pathological. For example, the husband would upbraid the wife for being unable to take initiative or control the housemaids. On the other hand, if she gave instructions to the maids, he would countermand her instructions in the presence of the housemaids, making her seem incompetent. As a result, she developed severe inhibitory tendencies and an entirely submissive disposition. In treatment, Mrs. S. J. moaned, "Why can't I have my own opinion or express my opinion, a graduate like me; why am I always the one that is wrong?"

Treatment consisted of joint marital therapy, with both the husband and wife attending the sessions, as well as assertiveness training for the wife. In a couple of months, the wife regained full health and became completely functional. Her physical symptoms disappeared. However, as the wife recovered, the husband became ill. He was rushed to the University of Nigeria Teaching Hospital, seventy kilometers away, with a suspected cardiac condition. After all the medical evaluations, his condition was diagnosed as psychological. He had no physical problem but was reacting to the improvement in his wife's health! He was referred back to us for treatment.

In this case, as in some other families we treated, the illness of the wife arose from the symbiosis within the family system in which one person exhibits pathology as a result of the improper (pathological) transactions (interactions) between family members. Psychologists have long recognized that mental-health problems (and their accompanying physical manifestations) can arise as a result of the way a person is treated by other family members. In this case, the husband's negative dealings with the wife caused her pathology. Improvement in the wife's condition allowed her become assertive; the husband felt that he had lost control and panicked, leading to his supposed cardiac condition. Further therapy with the couple reengineered the family dynamics so that the husband no longer would feel threatened by his spouse and children's increasing strength and independence and that the wife applies her new independence in a healthy manner. The husband recovered fully, and a healthy climate prevailed in the family, even after a ten-year follow-up assessment. A turkey at Christmas for several years was one of the ways they expressed their gratitude for our intervention.

Miss K. C.

Miss K. C. was twenty-four years, old. She was referred to our clinic for the treatment of multiple disabling phobic complaints and depression. She was afraid of the dark, of being alone, of open spaces, and of household pests, such as cockroaches and also earthworms. Seeing a cockroach would send her into a crisis and frenzy for a whole day. She would shiver, crouch in a corner of the bed clutching a Bible, and shout, "Blood of Jesus! Blood of Jesus cover me!" She would reject contact with close family members. The sight of a butterfly innocently flying by also would make her shout "blood of Jesus!" because the butterfly represented an agent of malevolent forces or people that had been sent to harm her. She had been in school and was doing well in her medical coursework but abandoned her studies when she became ill. She had been out of school for more than eighteen months when she was referred to our clinic. She had undergone a full medical examination, and there was no identifiable medical problem. She was referred to our clinic for psychological intervention after several efforts with traditional healers and faith healers.

Clinical assessment affirmed the various phobic conditions. There was also a high depressive component. The young lady scored high on intelligence, however. She also was very religious, ascribing her condition to the "work of the devil" and her cure as possible only with the proper intervention of God. She asked me repeatedly whether I was a pastor, a "man of God." It was clear that she would have preferred a man of God's intervention, even though she also complained that she had consulted many of them without success. She had feelings of guilt regarding her previous sexual encounters, and these guilt feelings were not assuaged by the various healing sessions, faith renewal crusades, and night vigils she attended.

Social assessment revealed that her family had an intense religious fervor, although various family members attended different churches: Roman Catholic, Anglican, and various denominations of the Pentecostal "born again" church. In fact, it was rare for two people to be part of the same congregation. There was also constant bickering within the family about who was worshiping the right way and who was not or which version of the Bible that was the correct or true bible. Religion was a point of conflict and discord within the family, rather than a source of cohesion. With such a discordant family system and with the mother and father each attending separate churches, there was hardly any effective parental influence and emotional support.

Engaging the young lady in psychotherapy was a long-drawn-out affair. She came to the sessions clutching her Bible and, in the initial phase, quoted copiously from it. She sought to incorporate biblical wisdom into the therapy sessions. One of the facts that emerged was that during her last two years of schooling, she spent more time reading her Bible than her medical textbooks. Most times, it didn't really matter what book of the Bible she turned to; any part of it was soothing.

It took considerable effort to engage her in the process of psychotherapy. Following six months of intensive psychological treatment, she regained her psychological health and was no longer subject to the phobias. She became sufficiently empowered to engage life in a proactive manner and returned to school. Indeed, she performed so well, she won a prize in surgery. She did not completely abandon the Bible but she relied on it in a more realistic and healthy manner. This was reflected in her assessment of her healing process. In a session close to the termination of treatment, she reasoned that it was God's will that physicians heal sick bodies and that spending her time reading her medical books and not the Bible was, in fact, doing God's will. It took quite some time for her to arrive at this balanced appraisal of religion and medicine, and we were pleased when she did. It was a turning point in her treatment.

The above case is only one of several that have passed through our clinic reflecting increasingly serious difficulties connected to extreme religiosity within the population. Fundamental religious leanings combined with traditional cultures—both of which ascribe responsibility for all events to God, the gods, the devil, malevolent forces, or wicked people—complicate the human need for personal empowerment, which enables people to take charge of events in their lives and make effective choices. Education needs to inculcate the understanding that people have the free will to order their lives. God, the devil, and wicked people must be overburdened with responsibilities in these days characterized by extreme "other attribution"! Fresh psychological expertise is needed to enhance treatment when faith becomes a hindering factor, rather than a healing force.

The above are cases that gladden the heart and make practice of the clinical specialty of psychology rewarding. Some conditions respond to drug treatment. But others require the specialized therapeutic skills of a psychologist. There is now sufficient awareness that a good number of the conditions being treated in hospitals are psychological or have psychological consequences for patients. An individual suffering from depression may respond temporarily to drug management, but the ultimate resolution often depends on reengineering the person's mental life so he or she can acquire better coping skills as well as the resolution of the social and personal conflicts that underlie various mental health conditions. In addition, the question of what actually heals the sick mind goes beyond techniques of therapy or medicines. Healing often arises from the relationship that is developed during psychotherapy, which allows the patient to experience deep empathy, warmth, and healing support from another human being in a non-judgmental atmosphere of self-exploration, self-understanding, self-change, and self-acceptance.

Chapter 19

Tales of a Grandfather

The children have been sources of immense joy for Susan and me. True, we lost two of them, Uchenna Felix and Arinzechukwu Stanley, but they too were great delight. The others, Adaeze Susan, Onyechi Leonard, Anayo Kenneth, and Ngozichukwu Lillian have been a blessing. We had no difficulties in their upbringing. When I left for the United States on diplomatic service for Biafra, they stayed with my mother, brothers, sisters and lots of aunties and uncles. Adaeze got into secondary school at Mary Mount College, Agbor, Delta State. She graduated and got into the University of Nigeria, Nsukka, my alma mater, majoring in mathematics. In 1972, Susan and the rest of the children, including Arinzechukwu, joined me in the United States. I was in school at the University of Miami in Florida. It was a wonderful experience. We made regular trips to fun places in Miami, including the well-stocked zoos, Disney World, the Seaquarium, the Serpentarium, Key West, Biscayne Bay, and the Coral Reefs and made regular fishing expeditions to Tamiami Trail and the Florida Keys, where we caught a variety of fish. We also went to the planetarium in Philadelphia. When Adaeze visited us in 1975, we had a long exciting motor ride from Coral Gables in Florida to Philadelphia in Pennsylvania, where I was to undergo my pre-doctoral internship. We also went up to New York and visited the Statue of Liberty. Those were fun times.

In raising the children, we had no special problems with discipline. Indeed we had no problems to speak of; our children all matured and started their own families' lives with no hitches. Susan and I consider ourselves truly lucky with the children God placed in our care.

Children will be children, of course, as evidenced by an early experience with Adaeze and her schoolwork. One day, she came back from school complaining that the teacher had flogged her. I asked why the teacher flogged her, and she said it was because she did not do her homework. It seemed she wanted her dear father, her strong and powerful father, to intervene with the monstrous teacher. (With children, all fathers are strong and powerful!.) At that time, the notion that parents could go and harass a teacher for disciplining their child was beginning to emerge, and Adaeze might have been aware of this attitude, exhibited by the up-and-coming middle class and the rich and powerful in society. However, I had grown up with the old fashioned culture that the teacher was right, even in administering punishment, and parents supported the teacher. I told my daughter that the teacher punished her because she was disobedient.

I asked Adaeze how many lashes of the cane the teacher applied, and she said four. I then told her that I would double that number, that is, I would give her eight lashes. I got a cane and asked her to stretch out her hand, and she did, so meekly, all the while looking into my eyes to see whether her loving father would in fact apply the punishment. I did, and although she winced and yelped at every stroke, she obediently kept her hands outstretched. By the time I got to the fourth whipping, with her eyes still trained on me, my heart gave way and I could not go on. I drew her to me and wiped her tears. My eyes were wet too. I believe she noticed. I told her not to make her daddy whip her ever again, which I would if she failed to do what the teachers asked her to do. She had no problems with school after that; in fact, she excelled, and I was happy not to flog my little girl ever again.

The grandchildren are in a special class all by themselves. I have already mentioned the glorious day my first grandchild, Uchenna Ngoddy, was born. Uchenna (God's will) is a unisex name in Igbo land. I believe that Adaeze, her mother, prevailed on her husband's family to give the baby the name in memory of her brother, Uchenna. I had no hand in that. Each of the other grandchildren has brought immense joy to Susan and me.

With grandchildren, the generational gap becomes even more obvious, as with music, for example. Their taste is for loud, blaring, ear-piercing sounds, and barely comprehensible (to me, incomprehensible) rap. The only time they spare you the noise is when there is a music player plugged into both ears. What is wrong with their eardrums? Have ears become less sensitive? The classical forms are not for them. Beethoven, Handel, Mozart, Tchaikovsky, and the like are not welcome guests in their music collections. I matured on the classical forms and warmed up to artists like Jim Reeves, Miriam Makeba, Elvis Presley, Lionel Ritchie, Tom Jones, Otis Redding, Ray Charles, Steve Wonder, the Beatles, Dolly Parton, and Michael Jackson, as well as, some reggae and old calypso tunes, such as those by Harry Belafonte, my man. I also enjoy soft jazz and music with comprehensible lyrics, heartwarming love songs, ballads, and sounds. And, of course, there is West African Highlife music from artists like the Ghanaian E. T. Mensah, my Atani compatriot, Steven Osadebe, and others. To the grandchildren, these are boring sounds. Their icons are the rap masters: 50 Cent, Eminem, Ludacris, and others. "Old school," they call me! Old-fashioned, they mean. Rap is good music, I am sure; it has to be based on its effect on my grandchildren, but why all the noise and speed? It reflects a new world that is in a hurry, but I can't figure out where everyone is going to! I concede that, now and then, I hear the young ones cooing and dancing to Michael Jackson's tunes ("We are the world"; indeed, it is their world) and to "African Queen" by the Nigerian artist Two-face. So perhaps there is hope, then.

The living room is a permanent battleground over music and television programs. I root for CNN and Sky News, but I am usually out voted in favor of the movie and sports channels, sometimes for twenty-four hours at a stretch! Their logic is enticing. They say, "Grandpa, what's in the news but fighting and conflicts all over? There's Liberia, Sierra Leone, Iraq, Lebanon, the Sudan, Nepal, the Congo, Afghanistan—so, so many wars. People *actually* killing people? At least what we watch is just make-believe. We know that nobody actually dies. The actors are alive."

Well, they do have a point. Does the news I watch change anything, they often ask. Doesn't the movie provide vicarious enjoyment, relieve tension, and allow for a harmless expression of various emotions, including hostility, with no enduring anxiety over the outcome? But I counter that they can't pass their examinations unless they know social studies, for example, the names of places, their governors, and even the president! And they won't find these in movies but on the radio or TV news and in newspapers. Because they wake up in the mornings bleary-eyed from too much visual strain and with headaches, occasionally, Grandpa has to put his foot down and shout "Bedtime!" or "No TV on schooldays."

Books have taken the back stage in the upbringing of children. It is truly a different world. I always have a series of newspapers and magazines around the house: *Time*, the Nigerian *Newswatch*, and other dailies. My children would have fought over who would be the first to read them, and sometimes one person would hide a copy in order to read it longer. Not anymore, not with most of the grandchildren. A few are bookworms, like Onyechi's daughter, Uju, and Adaeze's daughter, Nwamaka Ngoddy. Nwamaka is the other extreme; she has a book open whether she is at breakfast, lunch, or supper and has to be forced to eat her food! Kadizue, Onyechi's son, is a voracious reader who read *The Da Vinci Code* in about six hours, while also watching television programs now and again! In general, though, reading is now not a favored item in childhood activities. Television and the Internet have taken over. Very little attention is paid to the newspapers anymore; now I have them all to myself. I do miss the joy of shouting "Who has the *Time* magazine?" or "Who is hiding *The Guardian*?"

Of course, there is all the fun with the grandchildren. One experiences the fun of playing games with the grandchildren when they are around and letting them cheat you. One of them (name withheld) can manipulate the WHOT cards to his personal advantage right before your eyes or find a way to shake the checkers board to disorganize the pieces when the game is not going in his favor! But he also will tell you afterward, with glee and a gust of laughter, that he had gotten the better of you by the manipulation; which makes his childhood mischief less galling. The grandchildren have been so much fun. I make sure that all the available games are in my home—WHOT (a card game), Ludo, Scrabble, draughts, chess, and others—as these are sources of continuing exchanges, one-to-one encounters, and entertainment. By the way, in my practice of family therapy, I insist that families have these games in their homes and that such shared entertainment be part of their routine transactions, for recreation, tension relief, and more important, regular interpersonal communion. I also insist on this in premarital counseling to enhance couple interaction. I have also found that children improve their language and computational skills if they play these games regularly.

You can enjoy grandchildren without the direct responsibility and obligations of the day-to-day childcare, including changing diapers, except of course for Susan who goes for the *Omugwo* (early child care), the Igbo tradition of grandmothers residing with their daughters following childbirth. It is fun when we visit the children, or they visit us. I have had some exciting experiences with the grandchildren. At the age of five, Olisaemeka, the first of my son Anayo's children would pick up his father's cell phone to call me, usually only when he knew that his dad was taking a bath and would not be able to get the phone from him easily! I don't believe I was that sharp at his age.

Oly, the youngest of Lillian's girls, at five-plus years, had a way of asking questions that threw one off guard. One day she came up to me and said, "My Mom said you are my grandpa. What does a grandpa do?"

Now, how do you answer such a question? And really what do grandpas do?

I said simply, "Grandpas play with their grandchildren." Then I proceeded to throw her up and about in play. I couldn't think of a better response at the time. I can't think of one now! Chidimma, Amarachi, Uchechi, Lillian's other girls, are old enough to accept their grandpa without such questioning. And Emma, the youngest, is too young to ask.

AJ (Austin Junior) is Adaeze's son, with whom I played peek-a-boo fright games in their Atlanta home. He was about six years old. I would make monster faces at him, with a finger of each hand stuck in my ears, and make "frightening" movements with the rest of my fingers, accompanied by guttural sounds while I chased him all over the house. He would run away from me, seemingly scared. In the end, when I was thoroughly exhausted and lying prostrate on the sofa, he would come to me and say, "Grandpa, I wasn't really scared. Let's do it again, please. Come on, Grandpa, let's do it again." If I hesitated, he would urge me on saying, "Come on, Grandpa. You're not tired, are you?"

"Of course not." I would lie, trying to stagger back up. "This time I am going to scare you real bad!"

Wearily I would get up and start all over again, with my legs threatening to give up on me! His young and pretty sister Chi-chi, the third and youngest of Adaeze's girls, would watch us in amusement and sometimes say, "Leave Grandpa alone!" What grandpas have to go through! But you should see the endless hugs I got, and then when we were both tired and worn out, he would snuggle into my lap and sleep. And I would put him to bed and watch him sleep so peacefully, happy with his grandpa. Who would want to miss all that?

Onyechi's second son, Okwudili (Junior) had one on me. He sustained a sprain on his leg, and it was recommended that heat treatment be applied to the leg. I took on the task. He winced, yelped, and jerked his leg in apparent pain when I applied the treatment. Afterward he said, "Thank you, Grandpa," and limped away, nursing the leg I had just treated. A week later, I learned that as he limped away, he had a good laugh with his friends. He had given me the wrong leg and was play acting all the while I was busy treating the wrong leg!

Kadizue is the eldest of my son Onyechi's children. Once there was a primary school activity that he and his siblings (Okwudili. Jr. and Obi-Chukwu) had to attend. It was mandatory. Kadizue's parents were away, however, and so Susan and I had to take them to the event. I felt very proud of myself with my sports cap and clothes. We had a good time. I thought we represented his parents quite well. However, the next day, Kadizue came home from school in tears. We were living next door then, and so we had continuing interactions with Onyechi's children. The young boy was distressed. I asked what the matter was, and he said, "Some of the boys in school who saw you yesterday said that my father is an old man and that he will soon die. Grandpapa, is it true that you will die soon?"

"Of course not. Do I look like I'm dying? And why didn't you tell them that I'm your grandpa, not your daddy?" I asked.

"I told them but they won't believe me. They say I am lying," he said, looking dejected and miserable.

The father they saw was me, with my gray hairs. His anguish was obviously not only about having an old father but also about the possibility of my demise. Children can be hurtful to one another sometimes. He said that he made every effort to convince them that I was his grandfather, but failed. We did the best we could to console him and to reassure him that his grandpa, though old, was not about to die. We also made sure that his father attended all future events.

Some years later, when Kadizue was in his third year in secondary school, I took him in my car on an errand. On our way, I asked him, "Are you not worried that your friends will see us together and laugh at you for having an old father?" He laughed and said, "Don't mind them, Grandpa. They now know my father, but the truth is that they were jealous. None of them has a professor for a grandfather."

Growing up, new perceptions, different feelings. I am now invited to any activity in his school, and he shows unhappiness if I am unable to attend. When he takes me to the cybercafé to check my e-mail, he warmly introduces me as his grandpa to the staff and his friends. And he takes pride in guiding me through his new world, the world of the Internet.

Chapter 20

Epilogue

You know, if I had to do it all over again, I would do the same things. Like Arinzechukwu said to Susan and me before he passed away, I too would be an Uzoka all over again, with the same mom, dad, brothers, sisters, wife, and children. Perhaps I would ask for a bit more of the good things of the present sojourn and of subsequent sojourns! I have a great family, and life has been kind and exciting; watching civilization grow from the gramophone, the telegraph, and radio to television, DVDs, and music and film on the Internet, from landline telephones to the cell phone, and from prop planes to supersonic jets. The discovery of microchips has truly revolutionized the world of electronics beyond imagination. The fictional stories and imagined gadgetry of the 1940s and 1950s have become commonplace reality. To write my Ph.D. thesis, only thirty years ago, I spent hours on large-frame computers, writing and rewriting the input programs. Now, I carry along my laptop computer to the village and work away on my papers with unbelievable ease.

Man has walked on the moon; a space station has residents in place even as it continues to be developed; and space travel now approaches wide commercialization. The Japanese say they are working on humans being resident on the moon in less than two decades. Given the present march of science and technology, this is not considered overly ambitious. Medical science is not too far away from the day when individual hearts, lungs, kidneys and other organs will be grown outside the body in laboratories and implanted to replace diseased organs. The problems of donor source and organ rejection soon will be a thing of the past, mentioned only in passing in historical medical books. Indeed, the prospect of sending in special cells to repair damaged organs seems well within reach. And after creation of Dolly the sheep, human cloning has been held in check for moral reasons and perhaps due to the fear of unknown risks. All this is thanks to the emergence of embryonic stem cell research and other cutting-edge medical and surgical breakthroughs. If my father, who passed away in 1949, were to be resurrected today, he would be greatly puzzled and confused by the innovations that are now commonplace; he would even be lost in the modern maze of motor traffic. Today, the younger generation is better able to handle the newer technologies than are those of my age. Indeed, when you visit many homes and ask for some electronic gadget to be turned on, you will be referred to the little people who know what to do!

In my lifetime, nations and political systems have evolved. Post-tsarist rule and the Communist revolution, Russia has witnessed the dramatic and unbelievable dismantling of core Communism with capitalist structures now in place. Some say it was all thanks to Mikhail Gorbachev, but others say it was an evolution, a change waiting to happen. Even China is embracing capitalist economic practices. Marx and Engels must be turning in their graves. And Lenin's spirit must be hovering in despair in his ornate mausoleum. Dust to dust, Mother Earth, a welcome relief for Lenin? Britain, a stable democracy, has gone through significant changes; she relinquished her colonies, but retained continuing affinity with her former vassals through the agency of British Commonwealth of nations. Some raise the question of who profits the most in these post-colonial arrangements; the colonial masters, or the former colonies. Lately, the British Labor Party seemed to be sitting pretty in Westminster to the chagrin of Tory, until an unexpected Tory-Liberal coalition swept them out of power. Angela Merkel, from the former Communist East Germany, is the first-ever female German chancellor. What would Hitler think? Don't ask me. There are antagonists and protagonists who think he is still alive. (People live to be a hundred and twenty years and older don't they?) After the glory days of Charles de Gaulle, France appeared a hesitant international player, but is now embracing a global leadership position. And Europe is being blended into an evolving cohesion in an amorphous coalition called the European Union. We are witnessing increasing movement from small enclaves and countries, to emerging globalization.

America has emerged from the experience of World War II and survived the Cold War to become the world's only super power. America is evolving beyond its borders. Perhaps, more correctly, the world is evolving around America—American music, American fashion, American food, and American youth culture. And the grand design appears to be the exportation of American brand democracy, with 9/11 defining a new orientation in American national security and international alignments.

Postwar China is moving away from its radical Communist roots, through the vision of the newer leadership. China's latent economic power is now surging forward inexorably, and Africa is being drawn into its economic fold. Taiwan remains a thorn in Sino-American relations. The Korean peninsula is still a flash point of festering insecurity, decades after the presumed end of the Korean conflict. Countries in the Middle East remain in intractable conflict, to the distress of lovers of the Holy Land, Arabs, Jews, and Christians alike.

Africa moved from slavery to colonial rule to independence, guided by Kwame Nkrumah, Jomo Kenyatta, Nnamdi Azikiwe, Mwalimu Julius Nyerere, and others. Through brutal, corrupt and dictatorial leadership regimes of Uganda's Idi Amin, Central Africa Republic's Emperor Jean Bedel Bokassa, Sudan's Alba Bashir, there is hope of possible people emancipation and freedom as South Africa's Nelson Mandela represents. Africa has its first democratically elected female leader, President Ellen Johnson-Sirleaf of Liberia. My beloved country Nigeria is hanging on the fringes of neo-democracy in a tottering awakening after years of military bastardization, fraud, and corruption-driven misrule. A glimmer of hope now prevails as this great African country, blessed with boundless human and natural resources, seeks to find its feet and mend its ways in the new international climate, which demands transparency and accountability. In the new spirit of regional cooperation, as with the European experiment, the African Union has emerged to replace the impotent Organization of African Unity with hopes of achieving greater vibrancy and relevance. "Debt relief, fair trade" is the current war cry. And how about good governance as an overarching goal?

An African, Kofi Annan, succeeded Boutros Boutros-Ghali, another African, as secretary general of the United Nations. Both men acquitted themselves creditably in the service of the world body. The United Nations is in the throes of fundamental changes in the face of endemic world crises and its own internal incoherence. But everyone agrees that the United Nations is it, until humans can find a better alternative to dialogue.

I have my feet across two centuries, the early 1900s and the beginning of the 2000s. In my lifetime, great leaders have influenced history, science, and the arts. My favorites include: Mohandas Gandhi with his philosophy of non-violence; Albert Einstein and his revolutionary general theory of relativity, upping science way beyond Isaac Newton. William Shakespeare, the wordsmith, the quintessential storyteller, whose writing influenced me in the early days and still does today. There is Alfred Nobel, whose research helped give the world destructive weapons technology and who established prizes to advance science and technology and promote world peace. Nelson Mandela, an icon of our times, a man who transcended the base emotions of anger and revenge, despite the horrors of apartheid and his own personal experience with it, and showed us how valor can reside in forgiveness. By exhibiting compassion, humanity, and accommodation, Mandela demonstrated the inherent possibility of human coexistence even in the most troubled circumstances. He won for himself a well-deserved Nobel Peace Prize and the Truth and Reconciliation Commission he supported, has become an accepted vehicle of national healing. There is Sigmund Freud and his revolutionary psychoanalytic theory of the dynamics of the human mind. After Freud, humans looked closely in the mirror and became better informed about their innate drives and the incredible power of the unconscious.

The now ubiquitous and versatile computer owes its existence to Charles Babbage, Bill Gates, and the other computer whiz kids, who put the communications process on another pedestal, a real forward march for mankind. Frantz Omar Fanon's eloquent lament on the colonial experience— *The Wretched of the Earth, Black Skin, White Masks*—was a landmark statement. Nigeria's Chinua Achebe's masterful recreation of Igbo and African life ways and the disruptive effects of colonialism on African societies is acclaimed, and *Things Fall Apart, The Arrow of God, No Longer at Ease*, and others have become world masterpieces, celebrated in film and theater. Another great Nigerian author, Wole Soyinka, won the Nobel Prize for literature and gave the world enduring works like *The Man Died, Ake*, and *Myth, Literature, and the African World*, among others. He also portrayed a deep appreciation of the African world. I had the singular privilege of living at the same time as a great pope, John Paul II, whose godliness deeply touched people of different faiths. It surprised no one that his successor (Pope Benedict XVI) sought to beatify him soon after his death. Vox Populi, Vox Dei!

On the other side of the divide, there was Adolf Hitler, who is at the top of the list of leaders who defined evil for this age, bequeathing history with a horrendous world war and the inhumane blot of the Holocaust. Hitler and leaders like Joseph Stalin of Russia, Augusto Pinochet of Chile, Idi Amin of Uganda, Slobodan Milosevic of the erstwhile Yugoslavia, and Charles Taylor of Liberia ironically have helped nations to develop a universal conscience of a common humanity. Increasingly, nations and leaders cannot now operate with impunity without considering the distinct possibility of a human rights commission descending on them sometime in the future. Now, people have the luxury of a human rights commission, and special courts for crimes against humanity.

All these have been part of my life experience in an age of dramatic, fairylike, and fiction-like changes. Who could ask for more? True, the world is not yet at peace; unreasonable and senseless wars and conflicts still degrade and devalue human life and the nuclear threat still hangs over the entire earth. There is the serious problem of poverty, world-wide, and efforts at eradicating poverty seem so very feeble. There is also the persistence of old scourges like malaria and tuberculosis and the emergence of new and troubling afflictions, such as HIV/AIDS, bird flu (avian influenza), and swine flu.

There is the specter of an emerging religious divide fueled by fundamentalism with terrorism as its primary weapon, which is proving difficult to manage. The prevailing attitude is that it does not represent a fundamental conflict between the major religious tenets. We are being persuaded to agree. Is it a clash of civilizations then? Time will have the answer. There is an even more insidious threat: global warming, the effects of long years of human unkindness to Mother Earth, which is now destroying human life in the tsunamis, unusually harsh hurricanes, unwholesome weather, floods, and wind storms that are now repeatedly occurring in different parts of the world.

And at the core, there are problems with child rearing and parenting. The television and the World Wide Web, even more than the schools, are becoming the parents of the future. A real challenge for humans is to evolve appropriate ways of humanizing and socializing people in an age increasingly dominated by machines and electronic gadgetry.

I remain optimistic, nonetheless, that the human condition has good prospects of achieving a meaningful balance between national/ethnic orientation and the needs of the global human family. Indeed, haven't humans restrained themselves from using the nuclear option in the more than sixty years since Hiroshima and Nagasaki, choosing instead the long period of the Cold War? Rationality is alive and well. I am optimistic that concern for the poor of the earth will become top priority on the agenda of nations and the international community. I am also optimistic that a balance will emerge between personal greed and the public good, between use and abuse of the earth (the Kyoto protocol is only a beginning), between the role of machines and role of humans, between different faiths, and between faith and reason.

Did I say something about not being lucky, about never winning at sweepstakes? I have not won sweepstakes or lottery, that's true. No matter how many times I try, I just don't win. But I have been lucky, truly lucky in the important things. Is anything really possible without the gift of good luck, the endowment of God's grace? Yes, I worked hard; oh yes, I sure did. But some people work hard and fail to achieve results. Despite the hard times and having to work extra hard to earn anything, my careers and experiences have been rewarding. I would have loved to have been a great footballer, a great musician, a great surgeon—so many professions that hold strong appeal for me—indeed, a great everything, really. Well, maybe next time around!

Nevertheless, with seventy years behind me, I am comforted by the knowledge that life has been kind to me. Among a variety of gratifying things, I belong to a loving family (siblings, wife, children, and all) and have marvelous and enduring friendships. Again, my careers have been rewarding. I earned the fellowships of my primary intellectual and professional bodies and also the award of the Fellowship of the Social Science Academy of Nigeria, the academy I'd previously served as its president. In 1999, I was named alumnus of the year by the University of Miami. At the award ceremony, I delivered a paper titled "Psychology in Nigeria and Psychology's Global Agenda in the New Millennium." To cap it all, when I retired from Nnamdi Azikiwe University, I was honored with a distinguished service award and a new faculty staff office/student center building was named after me. During the event, with the state governor, Peter Obi, and the vice chancellor, Professor Ilochi Okafor (also senior advocate of Nigeria), present, my brother Okwudili instituted an annual cash award in my name that is granted each year to the best graduating student in the Faculty of Social Sciences. It was truly humbling, considering the tough beginnings and the travails of life. So, life has been kind, with a fair mix of the yin and the yang, and with God's grace discounting my many frailties, according me what I call "A Fair Share":

A fair share
Of life's fare
With toils and leisure
Pains and pleasure
Advances and retreats
Conquests and defeats
But always warmly engaged
In a process by Him decreed
Of growing up
From growing old.

As for "next time around," that is part of Igbo cosmology and belief systems. "I bia uwa ozo" or "I no uwa" mean reincarnation. It is about the return to the human world after death, a recycling of life journeys. Is it real? How do I know? Do you know any different, for sure? I tell my brother Okwudili that I would do it all over again under one condition, that is, that he would be the *Diokpala* then, not me. I tell him that we should take turns at the task and that he would fit the part admirably. And he tells me he would "dodge" it, meaning that he would evade the position. "There's nothing I can't dodge, if I want to," he says.

Can you believe the man? And I wonder: did he dodge it this time around? Well, I tell him I won't let him do any dodging, next time. We shall see.

Postscript

Barak Obama is more than a postscript. Indeed, he should be the preface to any book, especially one about the events of the new millennium. Perhaps I will write another book. By some quirk of circumstance, this book did not get published until after the Barak Obama phenomenon. Yes, phenomenon. Is this truly an age to beat all ages? Who would have thought that America had evolved to this level of democracy and humanism? Is it maturity, or is it realism in the face of the existing enormous challenges? Susan and I were in Atlanta during the final days of the elections, and we stayed up all night to hear Wolf Blitzer say on CNN that "Barak Obama has been elected the forty-fourth president of the United States of America." It was an electrifying moment in world and human history. It was fever pitch. I do not see the magic in the promise. The real magic is simply in the event itself, an event endorsing merit and excellence and manifesting the strength of the human spirit in a dispirited world. It was thrilling to observe the spontaneous outpouring of emotions, the applause, and the love across the globe from a grateful world, a hopeful world. Obama represents a new and refreshing American national orientation, fresh approaches to international relations, and respect for the dignity of the human person. Wow! Humans indeed can be hopeful in an era that has emerged from the audacity of hope.

Appendix I:
The Family We Have - Strictly for Family and the Family Minded.

Susan and I have a truly large family. Besides our immediate children, we have our extended families on both sides, and various other people's children have lived with us. Our immersion in this wide human network has been the main source of our good health and happiness. In the beginning, there were our parents, who nurtured warm relationships within their families and handed over a tradition of love to us the children. It is the same in my family as it is in Susan's family. Susan and her siblings (Eliza, Rosa, Livinus, and Ossai) have a tradition of meeting at least once a year to share felicitations and "fight" over meals as they did in their childhood. They rotate the meetings from one household to another in the different towns where they live. It is pleasant to see them, all older than fifty, "quarrelling" (actually, pleasantly arguing) over who is eating faster or getting the better part of the meal.

I too continue to enjoy the tradition of enjoying meals together, a tradition that our mother bequeathed to us. When we get to the village, Atani, the cooking is for everybody but accommodates individual idiosyncrasies, for example, my allergy to onions. All of us are past sixty and surrounded by some families in the town who do not even visit each other!

I also enjoy the warmth of my siblings' children. There are my sister Omebele-Anne's children: Bose, Maria, and Chioma (Ayo and Femi have passed on); Adaobi's boy, John; Okwudili's Chike Felix, Adaora, Ikenna (Ik-Bobo), Mukosolu Faith, and Ndalaku; Chukwuemeka's Nnena, Chinedu, Chioma, Chikodili, and Ijeamaka (I-J), "my wife." My sister Uzoamaka's children are Nneoma, Emeka, and Onyekachi.

The grandchildren are so much fun: Ada's Uchenna, Nwamaka, Chi-Chi, and Austin-Junior (A-J); Onyechi's Kadizue, Okwudili (Jr.), Obichukwu, and Uju Adaeze; Anayo Kenneth's Olisaemeka and Adaobi Somto; and Lillian's Chidimma, Amarachi, Uchechi, Oluchi, and Emmanuel Chukwuebuka.

Then, there are my Uncle Luke Chukwudebelu's children: Vicky, Okey, Chibogu, Ngozi-Florence, and Dubem. Uncle Ezeanwani's son is Nwachukwu, and Uncle Ulasi's Nonye, Ifeanyi, Olisaeloka, Nwizu, Nkechi and Anthonia. They are family, all family. Then there are the wives, so many wives! Does the

Diokpala have wives! Because I am the *Diokpala*, the head of the family, all my uncle's wives are my "wives." My brothers' wives, Okwudili's Genevieve and Chukwuemeka's Obiamaka, are also my "wives." And the children's wives—Onyechi's Ifeyinwa, Kenneth's Obiageli, Chike's Nkoli, and Nwachukwu's Chigozie—are all my "wives." It is quite a harem for a *Diokpala* who is past seventy, but thank God it's only in name, merely ceremonial.

Family love manifests itself in relationships that are downright funny but truly heartwarming. My son Onyechi's only daughter Uju-Adaeze, at age nine, reveled in being called the "wife" of my younger brother Okwudili and took the relationship quite seriously by being possessive. A similar relationship exists between my brother Chukwuemeka's youngest daughter, I-J, and me. Our relationship is truly interesting. At the age of five-plus, when this "marriage" began, I had sufficient gray hair to be recognized as old. She would come to my compound and straight to my room and spend time with me, telling stories. She was extremely bright for her age. And we would hold hands all the while. Many times she would insist that I carry her on my back, to the amusement of the people around. There is a photograph of us in that activity. Now, this sweet young girl said we would marry but that if I got much older and started using a walking stick, she should be free to marry another man. Of course, I readily agreed. I have tried not to use a walking stick in order to keep the marriage alive! At the celebration of Susan and my seventieth birthdays and the fiftieth anniversary of our wedding, after we had been rejoined again in matrimony by the officiating priest, Rev. Father Alexander Agbata, this wonderful loving girl came to me and took my hand. We walked away to go sit by ourselves and talk about the events of the day, indifferent to the continuing proceedings. It was as if she and I were the ones who actually got married.

My brother often tells a story about his youngest daughter, Ndalaku, who was then about seven years old. Ndalaku was called "my wife" by one old man named Ezugo, who was living by the riverbanks in Akili, my mother's town where Okwudili, Ndalaku's father, often went fishing and hunting. Okwudili is a good marksman and good at fishing also. He loves the village life. He had a warm relationship with the old man in whose house he kept his fishing and hunting gear and his motorized boat. Often, he took Ndalaku with him on these trips. One day, Ndalaku surprised her father by saying that Ezugo was rather old and that she would prefer to get another husband, a younger man. Her father told her to look around and indicate whom she would want for a new husband. With very little hesitation, she said she would prefer Onyechi, my eldest son!. The father told her that there was very little difficulty with that since it was all in the family, and that all he needed to do was to see me with the necessary customary drinks and kola nuts and obtain my consent. It would be quite inexpensive since soda was my preferred drink. Are we supporting incestuous marriages? No, this is just family love radiating innocently in the children who perceive affection among their relatives across family households and across all ages, a great heritage to cherish.

My brother Okwudili named his first son Felix, after me, and I named two of my grandsons after my brothers, Okwudili and Chukwuemeka. Uzoamaka-Stella again named her first son Chukwuemeka after her brother. My son Kenneth's daughter Adaobi-Somto is named after my sister Adaobi. Names of older family members are being perpetuated and celebrated in the grandchildren; expressions of affection and continuity.

Christmas is a period to which all the children of the family look forward. I guess the elders do too. Some of the children even want birthdays that occur earlier in the year to be celebrated at yuletide. During this period, there is so much family fun that the children and even the elders find very little interest in attending outside events. There is usually a family picnic at a waterfront with much eating and frolicking, and both the old and the young spattering around in the water. On these occasions, Ndalaku, Okwudili's youngest daughter, is in her element. She gets all the children ready and prepares the needed snacks. She is like a mother hen, shepherding the younger ones around. She is a whole bundle of affection.

Me and Mom

Susan

Adaeze-Susan

The children (Ken and Leonard-at back, Lilian
and Arinzechukwu-Stanley up front

Me and brothers - Okwudili left, and Chukwuemeka to the right

Anne

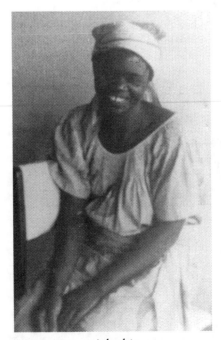

Adaobi

Kate

Stella

Family
Seated - Uncle Luke Chukwudebelu (extreme right), Me,
Susan with little Adaeze (center), Stella (left) and standing
at back - Okwudili at right, and Chukwuemeka - left

Hyacinth (left) and Me

How does one explain the love that my siblings and I have for each other? We have never had reason to ask someone outside the family to settle matters for us. When we have disagreements over matters, these are settled with reason on all sides. That is as it should be in a group of enlightened, caring people. It is not always so in all families, but we have the good fortune of a loving heritage that we have continued to nurture. This is not just within my immediate family, my siblings and me, but within our larger family nexus—uncles and aunts on all sides and many nephews and nieces. There is a spirit of giving that pervades our transactions, with no one wanting the other to be in undue distress. There is constant movement of financial and material resources across our different households as need determines. My brother Okwudili (Odi, as we call him), in particular, has generosity as his badge of existence, inside and outside our family. And the children have lived where they wished in our various homes as circumstances dictated. My son, Anayo Ken, stayed with my brother Chukwuemeka all through his law studies, and it was his home, at no expense to me. And because it is family, there is never a formal "thank you," just a knowing look and often a tender touch. My sisters, Omebele-Anne, Kate, Adaobi, and Uzoamaka, in their various ways, have provided the emotional bond that has kept the family in harmony. We all embrace each time we meet. We are an embracing family. We never tire of embracing one another. As the children mature, we enjoy seeing them making friendships across the family households. We inherited a loving, caring family and I feel happy that we still have the caring and loving disposition that we inherited.

Other people have added joy to the family by their presence in our midst. Other people's children, who have lived with us over the years, whether they are blood relatives or began their lives with us as household help, have made our lives joyful. One was Lawrence Onyeagoro. While in Owerri, we needed someone to assist with the chores and childcare. A number of children came forward, and I opted for Lawrence. Susan could not understand why I preferred Lawrence, a male, who looked ill and unkempt. Perhaps that was what got to my heart, because our first action was to get him to a doctor and treat his condition. Lawrence stayed with us when we moved to Enugu. In the meantime, we found out that Lawrence had not finished his primary education successfully, so we sent him back to school to finish and obtain his first school-leaving certificate. When he finished, I wanted him to go on to secondary school, but he preferred printing as a career, so I apprenticed him to a printing outfit. He acquired the training and skills to become employed at Alvan Ikoku College of Education in Owerri. That's the job he has held throughout.

Now, within a brief period of coming into the house, Lawrence became not just the help but also a family member. He became in all respects the senior brother of my children and was called Ndaa Lawly (Dear Big Brother Lawrence) by the children. Ndaa is a respectful appellation for an elder in Owerri Igbo dialect. He also became my friend and confidant. His wisdom was way beyond his age. And we too became part of his larger family in Emohe, Emii, which is near Owerri. The link was so strong that when the Nigerian Civil War broke out, his family invited Susan and the children to Emohe, a safer place of refuge. And Lawrence's family, especially his elder brother, gave succor to Susan and the children, giving them food and bush meat now and then.

Lawrence was honest beyond the ordinary. If I complained of being "broke," he would come up with some substantial amount of money to relieve my distress. Asked where he got the money, he would say that it represented change he had saved up from my pockets when taking my clothes to the cleaner! Admittedly, I am not very careful with money, especially loose change. Lawrence became a bank, my bank of last resort. A cousin of mine who was also living with us at the time never reported finding any money, even though he also took the wash to the cleaner from time to time. Lawrence brought love and warmth to the family. We shared the ups and downs of our family and his, his passing was a painful event for us.

Then there is Emilia Eluke (now Mrs. Emilia Madubuike), a bundle of love herself. Hardly ever moody, her laughter is infectious and her love of children is immeasurable. Children take after her like bees to nectar. Emilia is the daughter and only child of Susan's longtime close friend, Rose Obodo, who hailed from Oghe in Enugu State. Before Rose passed away, she placed Emilia in our care. Emilia, a serious-minded child, excelled in school and obtained a Bachelor of Science degree in estate management with second-class honors, upper division. She was the best overall student in her department for the year, with a performance that would warm any parent's heart. We wished that Rose, her mother, had lived to share in this joy. Emilia also won several awards and was recruited for a university teaching appointment. But she did not fancy being a teacher and took a bank job instead.

How does one describe the joy that this girl brought to the home? The young children in the home would be all over her. It was like mourning each time she had to leave, after holidays, to go back to school. Her trademark is a spontaneous laughter, with a lingering smile to amplify the warmth of the mood, and a deeply caring disposition. She has added warmth and caring to our lives and given more meaning to our lives. I was privately hoping that one of the boys in the family would marry her, but they had all become too much like brothers and sisters for that. I tried to marry her off to a cousin of mine, but that fell through too. Her wedding to Nnaemeka Madubuike was a celebration for my entire family.

Several people have lived with us, also becoming family. Obiageli Ogbo is my friend's daughter. Other people thought she was our daughter, and she even began to write her surname as "Uzoka" in her schoolbooks! Scholastica Ogochukwu Borlin and Emobe Cynthia Eyeye are Susan's nieces, and Adigwe Osakwe is my cousin on my mother's side; he is now an attorney. Onyechi Uwaechie, we call him Junior, is my grandson Kadizue's best friend. Good people, good human beings. So many people, young and old, have added fun and meaning to Susan's and my life, too many for complete mention. We do not fail to let them know that we have lived better because they gave so much of themselves.

Appendix II: Glossary

All words are Igbo unless indicated otherwise.

Ada (Adaeze): Appellation for every firstborn female child in the family

Aku: Tiny insect

Ala: Breast, mammary gland

Amosu: Witch or wizard

Bolekaja: *Yoruba.*- Derogatory term for a rickety vehicle.

Chukwu or Chukwu-Abiama: God, the Almighty

Dimkpa: Strong man

Diokpala: Appellation for a firstborn male child in a family

Egbe: Kite (small hawk)

Garri: Widely used term in Nigeria for a food item processed from cassava, much like grits

Igba-mgba: Wrestling

Ime: Pregnancy

Nna: Maggot, but if spelt with apostrophe (Nna') it means father

Ofuogoli: Derogatory term for an irresponsible person

Ogbe: A segment of a town, a quarter

Ugbugba: a clay pot used for cooking

Mkpulu-ji: Seed yam

Oku: Clay pot used for cooking

One-ime: Midwife

Omugwo: The practice in Igbo land, and perhaps in much of Africa, of mothers assisting their daughters with childcare after the birth of a baby

Okwuma: Shea butter, often used as a healing balm

Oyibo: Caucasian, male or female

Uhuru: *Swahili.* Freedom

Ute: Mat, usually made from raffia.

Umu-nwadiani: What Igbo families call the children of their sisters; nwadiani is singular